FINANCIAL FORTRESS

For Business Owners

FINANCIAL FORTRESS

For Business Owners

Extract Value through Entity Structure, Protection, Benefits, and Exit

Ira S. Koyner

Published by Triathlon Partners Media LLC

Triathlon
Partners
Media LLC

www.TriathlonPartners.com

ISBN: 979-8-9953718-2-3

Printed in the United States of America

IMPORTANT DISCLAIMER

This book is for educational purposes only. It is not investment, legal, tax, accounting, or insurance advice, and it is not an offer or solicitation of any service, product, or strategy.

The author is the founder of Triathlon Partners LLC, a registered investment adviser in the State of Connecticut and an independent insurance brokerage. The author and the firm may receive advisory fees or insurance commissions in connection with the kinds of structures discussed here and may have a financial interest in them. Registration as an investment adviser does not imply any level of skill or training.

All case studies, figures, projections, and policy illustrations are hypothetical and for illustration only. Actual results will differ. Insurance guarantees depend on the claims-paying ability of the issuer. Tax figures reflect federal law at the time of writing and change over time. State and local tax is generally not addressed.

Every structure in this book requires review by qualified legal, tax, and insurance professionals before implementation, and is not appropriate for all owners. A complete disclosure statement appears at the back of this book. Readers should read it.

Table of Contents

Preface: The Other Side of the Balance Sheet

For nearly thirty years, I traded foreign exchange options at large global banks. The work taught me that maximizing the profit from a trade required two things to be right.

The first was the idea itself.

The second was the structure the idea was expressed through. Structure is more than timing, size, entry, and exit. It is the platform underneath all of them. The structure was what produced the asymmetric payoff. It made more when the idea was correct and lost less when it was wrong. A good structure does not change the probability of success. It increases the degree of success and reduces the loss on each investment.

For the entrepreneur, the risk-return dynamic is different. A trader sizes each position so that small, frequent losses are overcome by larger wins, and treats failure as a routine cost of the next attempt. The entrepreneur does not get multiple attempts. There is one venture, and the owner lives with its outcome. A successful owner has spent years driving the probability of success as high as it will go. The challenge that remains is a different one: keeping and maximizing what the business has produced.

This capture happens, or fails to happen, in the structure underneath the business. Entity and liability protection keeps the personal balance sheet separate from the risks the owner has taken on. Continuity and ownership-transfer coverage absorbs key person events and partner exits without forcing a sale under pressure. Tax-efficient methods move wealth from the business balance sheet to the personal one. Estate planning is put in place years before it becomes urgent, because by the time it is urgent it is often too late. Each is a structural decision made in advance.

Together they determine how much of the business's success becomes personal wealth.

When I left trading and moved into financial planning, I expected to find the same discipline applied to the personal balance sheets of the business owners I worked with. I did not. What I found was fragmentation. One advisor managed the portfolio. Another filed the tax return. A third drafted the estate documents. A fourth sold insurance. Each was competent in their own lane. None of them coordinated across seams. The seams between specialists were where wealth quietly went missing.

My first book, *Financial Fortress: Building a Retirement Plan for Market Risk, Taxes, Inflation, and Life*, addressed that problem for households approaching or entering retirement.

This book applies the same thesis to a different audience. A retiree's wealth is liquid and quantifiable. A business owner's wealth is concentrated in a single illiquid asset, entangled with their income and exposed to risks portfolio theory does not model. The margin for error is smaller, the decisions less reversible, and the advisors more numerous and less coordinated.

Introduction

You are 56. You started the business 23 years ago with a partner. Fifteen employees, $11 million in revenue last year, $2.3 million in net income to you. The operating entity is an LLC formed in 2003 and never revisited. The buy-sell values the company on a multiple negotiated when revenue was a third of what it is now. The payroll company set up the 401(k) fifteen years ago. A personal guarantee signed at the 2019 refinance is still in place. Two of your senior people manage 60 percent of the client relationships. Your estate attorney isn't aware of the business's growth. Each advisor is good at their specialty. None of them talks to the others.

The plans you have are a patchwork assembled over twenty-three years. Made in isolation, they left money on the table. Each decision was appropriate at the time. This book shows how coordinated decisions move more of that money to your personal balance sheet.

Most business owners' wealth does not live in bank accounts. It lives in the enterprise: receivables, inventory, goodwill, equipment, brand, client relationships. On paper, the balance sheet may look substantial. The wealth is concentrated and the business is illiquid. This is an achievement and an obstacle at the same time.

What the balance sheet does not show are the retained earnings with no efficient distribution plan, the personal guarantee that exposes the household to a business event, or the retirement plan saving a fraction of what a better-designed one could.

The coordination is not primarily between advisors. It is between decisions. The entity choice interacts with retirement plan design, which interacts with the benefit structure, which interacts with the exit and estate planning. Each decision evaluated alone produces its own answer. Evaluated together, they produce a better one. Building the business and capturing the wealth are two different jobs. You have already accomplished the first. This book is about the second.

This book is structured around the four channels by which a business owner moves value out of the company and onto the personal balance sheet. Cash distributions. Continuity and protection. Benefit extraction. Exit strategy and estate planning. Each act addresses one of them.

The Four Channels

Value moves from the business to the household four ways. Each act covers one.

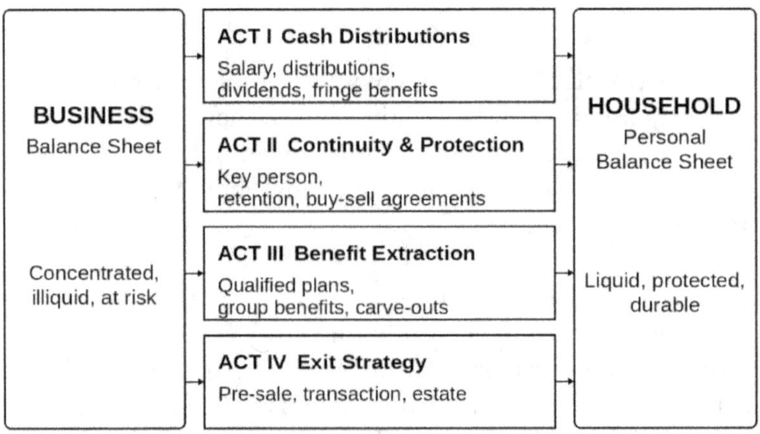

The entity underneath determines how efficiently each channel carries value across.

Concentration is the condition that makes the channels matter; structure and coordination determine how much of each one's value reaches the owner. The capstone at the end of each act shows the structures working together. Sonia. Donald and Gil. Dominique. Solomon.

If you want the coordinated plan that captures the maximum of what your business produces, keep reading. If you want a list of personal expenses to push through the business, a thicker stack of deductions on the same return, or the kind of nested trust structures sold in seminars, read something else.

The eight questions below are the topics that require coordinated analysis to find the right answer for your business. Any answer decided in isolation is worth revisiting. The case studies that follow show how integration produces the better result.

1. Entity reviewed in the last two years?
2. Key person coverage on every revenue-driver?
3. Buy-sell funded with current valuation?
4. Written retention structure?
5. Qualified plan designed for the business today?
6. Benefits running through the business?
7. Life insurance outside the taxable estate?
8. One advisor reviewing all of it together?

The book is built to be read in order. The concepts compound, and the capstones depend on the chapters before them.

Reading This Book Your Way

Throughout the book, several recurring callouts signal specific types of content:

Early Decision Rule: the principle that frames the chapter. Read these even if you skim.

Reality Check: a direct challenge to a common assumption. Intentionally blunt.

Rule Extracted: the lesson distilled from a case study or example.

What This Means for You: the practical takeaway translated from a case study into your own planning.

Design Choice Checkpoint: a decision point where the right answer depends on the specific business, not a universal rule.

Ask Your Advisor Today: questions designed to be brought verbatim into a planning meeting. If your advisor cannot answer them clearly, that is useful information.

Integration Check: the questions that close each act, connecting decisions across chapters into a single coordinated review.

The callouts are signposts. The chapters do the structural work in between.

ACT I: Cash Distributions

Cash moving from the business to the owner is where wealth actually transfers. Everything else in the book is built on making that transfer efficient. The entity decision dictates which channels are available and what each one costs to use. Yet the structure chosen at formation often no longer fits the business as it grows. Reinvestment, benefit utilization, and exit horizon each push the choice in a different direction. A business owner in the wrong entity pays more to move wealth and keeps less of it.

Chapter 1: Concentrated Wealth

The business that built the owner's success is also the single largest risk to it. The same capital and effort, concentrated in one operating entity, are what produced the wealth and what leaves it exposed.

> **Early Decision Rule**
> The business that produced the wealth is not necessarily the right place to hold it.

The Two Financial Realities

Every business owner lives in two financial worlds: the business and the household. Personal life continues regardless of what happens to the business.

The household runs on cash flow, not enterprise value. A business valued at $12 million that produces $4,000 a month in take-home pay is unbalanced. The owner may be a millionaire on paper and cash-poor in practice. Business equity cannot pay the mortgage, fund college, or cover a medical emergency unless it is converted into personal cash flow.

The Forms of Concentration

The concentration of capital and focus is what made the business successful. As it continues to grow, the personal balance sheet increasingly relies on the business balance sheet and assumes unnecessary risk that can be mitigated. That concentration shows up in three places.

1. Wealth concentration: the household balance sheet depends on a single illiquid asset.
2. Key person concentration: among dozens or hundreds of workers, only a small group drives the revenue, and the owner is usually one of them.
3. Ownership concentration: the business cannot be divided, sold, or transitioned without an agreement among co-owners that executes on its own terms.

Each form of concentration is addressed by one or more of the book's four channels. The channels are how the wealth, the people, and the ownership get moved, protected, or made liquid before the risk materializes.

Piercing the Corporate Veil

Forming a corporation or LLC creates a legal barrier between the owner and the business. Piercing the corporate veil is the legal doctrine that allows a court to ignore that barrier when the owner has failed to treat the business as a separate entity. When that happens, the liability that was supposed to stop at the business can pass through to the owner's personal assets. The entity may exist on paper, but if it is not operated as a separate business, the protection can disappear when it is needed most. The behaviors listed below can be perceived as piercing the corporate veil.

Commingling of Funds: No separation between business and personal bank accounts. Business funds flow to the owner without documentation, without a salary, without a distribution resolution. Personal expenses are paid with business funds. If the owner does not respect the separation, the legal system will not either.

Undercapitalization: The entity was formed with inadequate capital to conduct its business and meet its foreseeable obligations. The standard is that the business has to be funded in proportion to the risks it undertakes. Adequate insurance counts as capitalization.

Failure to Observe Corporate Formalities: Corporations are required to hold annual meetings, keep minutes, elect officers, and maintain records of major decisions. LLCs have fewer formal requirements but still need to follow their operating agreements and document member decisions. The formalities serve as evidence that the entity is real.

Multi-Entity Structures: Many business owners operate through a holding company at the top with separate LLCs for each project, property, or business line underneath. The structure provides liability isolation only if each entity is treated as a separate business. Separate bank accounts, proper operating agreements, adequate capitalization, arm's-length transactions between related entities, separate books, and tax returns are required for each.

> **Reality Check**
> The entity is a behavior, not a wall. The court tests the behavior, not the filing.

Personal Guarantees: The Voluntary Bridge

The corporate veil protects the owner from the business. The personal guarantee does the opposite. Most owners have signed at least one, on a commercial lease or a line of credit, and entity protection stops at the signature line. When guaranteed exposure exceeds the owner's liquid assets outside the business, it reverses the very protection the entity was formed to create.

The Owner's Vehicle

The vehicle purchase is the most common behavior that erodes the corporate veil. The owner purchases a luxury car through the business but uses it mostly for personal reasons. The accelerated depreciation is taken as a tax deduction. The deduction that looked like a financial windfall dissolves the protection the entity was established to provide. This commingling creates a liability for the personal balance sheet, as the separation between the owner and the business no longer exists. If an accident occurs, the assets of both the business and the household are exposed.

An additional cost is liquidity. Capital that could have stayed available, or been deployed more efficiently, is now locked in something that loses value every year. Liquidity is a valuable commodity to a business owner. It is needed to pursue opportunities, make a key hire, or fund an unexpected event, none of which a depreciating vehicle can support. The same pre-tax dollars deployed through the structures in Acts III and IV can produce an equivalent deduction with an asset that grows and remains accessible. The cash flow does not change, and the personal balance sheet is preserved and strengthened.

> **What This Means for You**
> The veil protects the owner only if the business is run as a separate entity. A personal guarantee punctures it voluntarily. The vehicle blurs it quietly.
> Each is a choice, and each one is reversible before the lawsuit arrives.

The next chapter covers how each entity structure affects taxes, benefits, and the path for moving value to the personal balance sheet.

Ask Your Advisor Today

1. Is every entity in my structure adequately capitalized and insured for the risks it undertakes?
2. Do I have separate bank accounts for every entity, with money moving between them under proper documentation?
3. If a plaintiff subpoenaed my bank records tomorrow, would they find commingling?
4. What is my total personal guarantee exposure, and is it greater than my liquid assets outside the business?

Chapter 2: The Entity Decision

Value moves from the business to the owner's personal balance sheet four ways: salary, pass-through distributions, dividends, and fringe benefits. Each is taxed differently, and the entity structure determines which are available and what each one costs to use. The entity is either an asset that lowers the cost of the transfer or a liability that raises it.

Most businesses start as LLCs. Easy, inexpensive, and usually the best decision in year one. As the business grows, three other structures become relevant.

> **Early Decision Rule**
> The structure that fit at formation is rarely the structure that fits at scale.

The Four Structures

Single-Member LLC
A liability wall sits between the owner and the business, but for tax purposes the wall does not exist: the IRS treats the LLC and the owner as the same taxpayer, and net profit flows straight to the owner's personal return.

Every dollar of that profit carries two taxes, income tax and self-employment tax. Self-employment tax is the owner's version of Social Security and Medicare. A W-2 employee splits the cost with the employer. The single-member LLC owner pays both halves. The combined rate is 15.3 percent up to the Social Security wage base of $184,500 in 2026. Above that, the 12.4 percent Social Security portion drops off and only the 2.9 percent Medicare portion remains. An additional 0.9 percent Medicare surtax applies above $200,000 single or $250,000 married filing jointly. The surtax is paid only by the earner, not matched by the employer.

Multi-Member LLC / Partnership

Two or more owners. The entity files its own return and issues a K-1 to each member. Self-employment tax treatment is the same as the single-member LLC. Every active member pays both halves on their share of ordinary business income.

What changes from the single-member LLC is governance. An operating agreement establishes ownership percentages, compensation terms, and continuity planning.

S-corp

What changes from the LLC is how payroll tax applies. The S-corp is a tax election, not a separate entity type. The owner draws a W-2 salary that must be reasonable for the role and supported by industry data. Payroll tax applies only to the salary. Remaining profit passes through as a distribution and is taxed as ordinary income, but avoids Social Security and Medicare tax. On the same business profit, the total payroll tax is lower than the LLC's.

C-corp

What changes from the S-corp is that the corporation becomes its own taxpayer. The corporation pays a flat 21 percent on its profits. When those after-tax profits are distributed as dividends, the owner pays personal tax at the qualified dividend rate of 18.8 or 23.8 percent depending on income level. On full distribution, this double layer often produces more total tax than the LLC or S-corp. That is the math most owners run. It is also the math that ends most C-corp conversations before they reach the real questions. What those conversations miss is that the C-corp is the only structure in which the full range of fringe benefits, health insurance, disability, long-term care, and group life, is both deductible to the corporation and excluded from the owner's personal income.

The Pass-Through Deduction (Section 199A)

The owner of an LLC, partnership, or S-corp can deduct up to 20 percent of qualified business income before tax. The C-corp gets no equivalent. The deduction applies every year, not once at sale.

Eligibility is based on the owner's total taxable income, not the business's income. Below the income threshold, every pass-through gets the full 20 percent. For 2026 the threshold is $403,500 for married couples filing jointly, half that for single filers, indexed to inflation. Above it, the rules are split by business type. A business is capped based on the wages it pays and the cost basis of its property and equipment. A professional-service business, including law, accounting, medicine, consulting, financial services, and brokerage, my own firm among them, sees its deduction shrink across the band above the threshold until it disappears entirely at $553,500, half that for single filers.

For most businesses the deduction is annual tax savings that belong in any entity comparison. A service business that no longer qualifies for the deduction should consider an entity change, since the C-corp's flat rate and deductible benefits do not depend on business type. The deduction is one input to the entity decision, weighed against the reinvestment, benefit, and exit differences between the structures.

> **Reality Check**
> The 20 percent deduction comes with limits. Above an income threshold it shrinks, and for a high-earning service business it disappears.

The Comparison That Misleads

A side-by-side at full distribution makes the C-corp look like the worst structure. Take a business with $400,000 in net profit and $150,000 owner salary.

($ in thousands)	LLC	S-Corp	C-Corp
Business Profit Before Owner Compensation	$400.0	$400.0	$400.0
Owner Salary	N/A	$150.0	$150.0
SE / Payroll Tax	$33.6	$23.0	$23.0
Corporate Tax (21%)	—	—	$50.1
Distribution / Dividend	$400.0	$238.5	$188.4
QBI Deduction	$70.2	$47.7	—
Federal Income Tax	$53.7	$60.3	$47.9
Total Federal Taxes	**$87.3**	**$83.3**	**$120.9**
Cash in Pocket	**$312.7**	**$316.7**	**$279.1**

All figures federal only. Married filing jointly, 2026 rates. State and local taxes not included. The C-corp scenario assumes all remaining profit is distributed as qualified dividends.

Profit Before Owner Compensation is the operating profit available before any owner salary, distribution, or payroll tax. The LLC scenario treats the full amount as distribution subject to self-employment tax. The S-corp and C-corp scenarios split it into reasonable W-2 compensation plus a distribution or dividend. Both pass-throughs are below the QBI income threshold and receive the full 20 percent deduction; the C-corp does not qualify for it.

On those numbers the S-corp puts the most cash in the owner's pocket. The C-corp puts the least. Every dollar of profit was distributed and double-taxed.

> **Reality Check**
> Most owners rule out the C-corp on the dividend comparison. They never run the comparisons that matter: benefits, reinvestment, and exit.

What the Distribution Table Misses: How Money Actually Moves

The distribution table assumes every dollar of profit leaves as a dividend. That is the worst-case assumption for a C-corp. In practice, value moves four ways. The mix determines the after-tax result, and two owners with the same profit can end up with different outcomes depending on how they use them.

The Four Ways Value Moves to the Personal Balance Sheet

Salary

Salary is deductible to the business and taxed once at the owner's marginal rate. The IRS can challenge salaries that are too high (treating excess as disguised dividends) or too low (treating shortfall as distribution avoidance). Salary also determines retirement plan contribution limits and eligibility for group benefits.

Distributions (Pass-Through Entities)

In every pass-through, business income is taxed to the owner as ordinary income whether it is distributed or left in the business, and the distribution itself is never taxed a second time. What differs is payroll tax. In an LLC or partnership, the active owner pays self-employment tax on the full share of ordinary income, so there is no portion that escapes it. In an S-corp, only the owner's salary carries payroll tax; the remaining profit passes through as a distribution free of Social Security and Medicare tax. That gap is the S-corp's payroll tax savings.

Dividends (C-Corp)

Dividends are not deductible to the C-corp. The corporation's earnings are taxed at corporate rates. When those earnings are distributed to the owner as dividends, they are taxed again at the individual level. This is the outcome shown in the distribution table. It is the least efficient way to extract value and is typically used only after other channels are maximized.

Fringe Benefits

Fringe benefits are where the comparison changes most. In a C-corp, many benefits are deductible to the business and excluded from the owner's personal income. In an S-corp, owners of more than 2 percent must include these benefits as taxable compensation. LLC owners generally receive no equivalent deduction. The C-corp benefit structure includes:

- Retirement plan contributions
- Group term life insurance
- Disability insurance
- Long-term care insurance
- Health insurance

Retirement plan contributions are a corporate-level deduction. The C-corp opens design choices that are awkward or unavailable in pass-through structures. Non-qualified deferred compensation, executive bonus arrangements, and supplemental retirement plans each work cleanly in a C-corp because the deduction stays at the entity level. Chapter 8 covers these structures in detail.

What Changes the Outcome

The four ways above describe how value leaves the business. Three of the C-corp's advantages decide how much of it the owner keeps, and they do not apply equally. One applies every year. One applies only with the right behavior. One applies only at the end.

Benefits (Universal Advantage)
Benefits are the only one of the three that does not depend on what the owner does. The deductible, tax-advantaged benefits listed above apply every year, whether the business grows, reinvests, or sells. That makes them the most consistent of the three advantages.

Reinvestment (Conditional Advantage)
Profits retained inside a C-corp are taxed at 21 percent. The same profits in a pass-through are taxed at the owner's personal rate, up to 37 percent, whether or not they are distributed. The spread compounds. More capital stays inside the business.

The advantage depends on behavior. Owners who reinvest benefit. Owners who distribute everything do not.

Exit (Situational Advantage)
The mechanics of an exit transaction (how proceeds are paid, when gain is recognized, what structures shelter the gain) depend on the entity. Chapter 9 covers the pre-sale structures in detail.

> **Reality Check:**
> Ask three professionals and you will get three answers. The CPA says stay an S-corp and keep the payroll tax low. The attorney says the LLC is cleaner to govern. The insurance advisor says the C-corp unlocks the benefits and the exit. None of them is wrong, and that is the problem. They are answering three different questions, and none of them was asked the one question that counts, which is what the business needs to do over the next ten years. That is the question no single specialist owns.

> **Design Choice Checkpoint**
> The distribution table answers the wrong question. The right question is which structure best moves income and value in the way that aligns with the owner's goals.
> - If the objective is to minimize payroll tax → salary and distributions dominate (S-corp)
> - If the objective is to maximize reinvestment or capture fringe benefits → C-corp
> - If the objective is exit optimization → entity structure determines what is possible

The entity is not just a tax classification. It is the system that controls how value leaves the business.

The Holding Company Structure

Owners with multiple projects, properties, or business lines often need more than one entity. A C-corp holding company on top of LLC subsidiaries combines liability protection with reinvestment capacity. The owner becomes a W-2 employee of the C-corp. Fringe benefits flow through it. Each project or property sits as a separate LLC underneath for liability isolation. The C-corp pays the salary, funds the retirement plan, pays the insurance premiums, and retains earnings at 21 percent for reinvestment across the subsidiaries.

The builder who has already formed a new LLC for every project is doing the liability isolation. The question is what sits above those LLCs. If the answer is the owner personally, every dollar of project income is taxed at the owner's marginal rate before it can be redeployed. A C-corp on top changes the math without changing operations.

When to Switch

Entity type is not a one-time decision. The structure that fit at formation often stops fitting as profit grows, reinvestment increases, and the owner's objectives shift. The change is usually gradual, which is why it is often missed.

A review is warranted when one or more of the following is true:

- Profits have reached a level where tax differences between structures matter
- A larger portion of earnings are being retained or reinvested
- Benefits are being paid personally instead of through the business
- The owner's focus shifts from income to long-term value or exit
- The business has grown in complexity, with multiple activities or entities

These are normal stages in the life of a successful business. When they occur, the original structure should be reconsidered.

Rule Extracted
Entity choice belongs on a two-to-three-year review cycle, and on any year revenue, income, or strategic direction hits an inflection point.

The entity structure that fits the business gives every chapter that follows a strong foundation. The buy-sell, the retirement plan, the benefit structure, and the exit all sit on top of it. If the entity is not an asset at the business's current size and stage, it is a liability that reduces ownership value.

Ask Your Advisor Today

1. What am I paying annually in payroll or self-employment taxes, and how much of that would I save under a different structure?
2. Am I leaving benefits or deductions on the table because of how the business is organized?
3. If I am planning an exit in the next five to ten years, does my current structure give me the best after-tax outcome on a sale?
4. Am I extracting capital from the business in the most tax-efficient combination of salary, distributions, and benefits?

Integration Check: Closing Act I

1. Has my entity been reviewed against current income, retained earnings, fringe benefits, and exit timeline in the last two years?
2. Are my multiple entities legally distinct in practice, not just on paper?
3. Have my personal guarantees been quantified against my liquid assets outside the business?
4. Is the entity structure ready to support the buy-sell, qualified plan, and group benefit structures in the chapters that follow?

ACT I CAPSTONE: Sonia, the Entity Decision

Sonia runs a bagel and bialy bakery in its seventh year. She grew up in Brooklyn working in her great-uncle Norman's bakery, learning to shape bialys from a recipe his family carried out of Bialystok. She moved to Springfield in her early thirties and could not find a proper bagel. She started baking on weekends, sold at the farmers market, and grew the operation into a storefront and supplying local restaurants and coffee shops. Net profit is $400,000. She formed an LLC at inception and hasn't re-evaluated since. Three things have changed.

Scenario One: The Annual Comparison
Sonia's profit and salary match the Chapter 2 example. The one change is that the pass-through deduction is now applied to the LLC and S-corp columns. Her bakery is an operating business, not a service business, and her taxable income sits below the phase-in threshold, so she takes the full 20 percent with no wage-test reduction. The C-corp gets no such deduction.

($ in thousands)	LLC	S-Corp	C-Corp
Business Profit Before Owner Compensation	$400.0	$400.0	$400.0
Owner Salary	N/A	$150.0	$150.0
SE / Payroll Tax	$33.6	$23.0	$23.0
Corporate Tax (21%)	—	—	$50.1
QBI Deduction (Section 199A)	$70.2	$47.7	—
Distribution / Dividend	$400.0	$238.5	$188.4
Federal Income Tax	$53.7	$60.3	$47.9
Total Federal Taxes	**$87.3**	**$83.3**	**$120.9**
Cash in Pocket	**$312.7**	**$316.7**	**$279.1**

All figures federal only. Married filing jointly, 2026 rates. The pass-through columns apply the full 20 percent Section 199A deduction; Sonia's taxable income is below the phase-in threshold and the bakery is not a service business, so neither the wage test nor the service-business exclusion reduces it. The C-corp scenario assumes all remaining profits distributed as qualified dividends. State and local taxes not included.

Add the pass-through deduction and the gap widens. On one year, the C-corp still looks like the loser.

A single year is the only frame in which it does. The S-corp leads the LLC by about $4,000 and beats the C-corp by roughly $38,000 on the one-year picture. But the entity decision is not a one-year decision. Sonia is reinvesting some of her profit, paying for benefits she could be deducting, and building toward a sale.

Scenario Two: Reinvestment Over Five Years

Assume Sonia reinvests $150,000 of revenue each year. As a pass-through, that $150,000 is taxed at her 37 percent marginal rate before she can deploy it. As a C-corp, the same profit is taxed at the corporate rate of 21 percent. Both grow at 15 percent inside their respective entities.

One year's reinvestment, valued at Year 5:

	LLC / S-Corp	**C-Corp**
Revenue assigned for reinvestment	$150,000	$150,000
Tax on retained profit	37% = $55,500	21% = $31,500
Capital available to reinvest	$94,500	$118,500
Value at Year 5 (15% growth)	$190,073	$238,346
Growth on Reinvestment	$95,573	$119,846
Tax on growth	37% = $35,362	21% = $25,168
Post-tax value	$154,711	$213,178
Tax on dividend (LTCG + NIIT)	—	$40,078/ $50,736
Net to owner at Year 5	**$154,711**	**$173,101/ $162,442**

Both C-corp columns assume the owner is above the $250,000 MFJ MAGI threshold for the 3.8% Net Investment Income Tax. The slash separates two qualified dividend outcomes: 15% long-term capital gains bracket first (18.8% effective with NIIT), 20% bracket second (23.8% effective with NIIT). The 20% bracket applies to taxable income above $613,700 MFJ in 2026. Pass-through profit is taxed at the owner's ordinary rate as allocated. Returns are illustrative, not a forecast. The 15 percent assumption represents reinvestment into the operating business and is not a portfolio return.

Keep profit inside the C-corp and it compounds on 79 cents of every dollar instead of 63. Five years is barely long enough to see it. The retention spread is 21 percent against up to 37 percent. Over five years the compounding gap shows up at the end.

Scenario Three: Reinvestment Over Ten Years
A successful business does not reinvest in itself once. The longer the horizon, the wider the gap. The same $150,000 of annual reinvestment, the same 15 percent growth, run for ten years:

	LLC / S-Corp	C-Corp
Annual revenue reinvested	$150,000	$150,000
Tax on retained revenue	37% = $55,500	21% = $31,500
Annual capital reinvested	$94,500	$118,500
Total Capital Deployed Over 10 years	$945,000	$1,185,000
Value at Year 10 (15% growth)	$2,206,507	$2,766,889
Profit at Year 10	$1,261,507	$1,581,889
Tax on profit	37% = $466,757	21% = $332,197
Post-tax value	$1,739,750	$2,434,692
Tax on dividend (LTCG + NIIT)	—	$457,722 / $579,457
Net to owner at Year 10	**$1,739,750**	**$1,976,970 / $1,855,236**

Same assumptions as Scenario Two; illustrative only.

The C-corp started behind on annual taxes and won anyway, because money left inside it grew on a 21 percent haircut instead of 37, and that spread compounded for ten years. This is the case the one-year table cannot show. Across ten years of reinvestment the C-corp delivers more to Sonia's personal balance sheet than the pass-through.

The analysis above assumes all value is eventually distributed. A sale of the business changes the calculation. Section 1202, the Qualified Small Business Stock (QSBS) rules, can reduce taxes on a substantial portion of the gain on qualifying C-corp stock. Chapter 9 covers the mechanics and limitations.

The Annual Cost of Staying an LLC

The reinvestment math runs on a five-to-ten-year horizon. There is also an annual cost that has been showing up on Sonia's personal tax return for seven years.

Sonia pays for family health insurance personally. As an LLC owner she cannot run it through the business as a deductible employee benefit, but a C-corp owner-employee can. The same is true for disability, long-term care, group term life, and retirement plan contributions. Each is deductible to the corporation and excluded from her personal income. (Chapter 7 covers the tax treatment of each benefit by entity type, with dollar figures.) Each is taxable W-2 compensation to the S-corp owner with more than 2 percent of stock. Each is non-deductible at the personal level for the LLC owner. At her marginal rate the gap is meaningful, and Chapter 7 puts the dollar figures on each benefit.

None of these benefits depend on growth, reinvestment, or an exit. They apply every year the entity continues.

Sonia's Decision

Sonia runs the three scenarios and the benefit math. The structure that suited her at formation, when profit was low and every dollar went to family needs, is no longer the structure that suits her at $400,000 in profit before owner compensation with reinvestment ambitions, an unfunded benefit menu, and a sale on the horizon.

She converts to a C-corp. The decision rests on three factors working in combination: annual benefit deductions, sustained reinvestment of retained earnings, and Section 1202 QSBS exclusion on a sale of the business. The conversion costs her the pass-through deduction Scenario One showed. That is the price. QBI is a deduction on annual operating income. QSBS can eliminate the federal tax on millions in gain at the sale she is planning in five years. The same horizon that makes the annual deduction add up is the horizon that delivers the exclusion, and the exclusion is worth multiples of the deduction. None of the three C-corp factors is sufficient on its own. Together they outweigh both the dividend penalty and the QBI deduction. This is the kind of trade only a coordinated plan surfaces.

> **Rule Extracted**
> An entity change decision requires analyzing many variables. A comparison built on one year of income misses the reinvestment, benefit, and exit strategies that can favor conversion.

ACT II: Continuity and Protection

Cash flow only reaches the owner if the people and the ownership structures producing it stay intact. Death, disability, voluntary departure, and partner exits each threaten that continuity. Each is rare in any given year. Each is certain across the life of a business. The owner who plans for them in advance keeps the business running through the disruption. The owner who does not is unprepared and jeopardizes the business's survival.

Chapter 3: Operational Continuity

Every business has one or two people the business cannot run without. One of them does not show up Monday. Not because they quit. Because they died over the weekend, or had a stroke. A key person is the one whose death or disability would damage revenue, client relationships, or operations the day it happens. The damage is identifiable, the cost is quantifiable, and the financial impact is insurable.

> **Early Decision Rule**
> Title and salary identify the org chart. Revenue at risk identifies the key person.

Key Person Risk

The revenue stream, institutional knowledge, and client relationships of a business are often concentrated in a small group of people. Replacing one requires capital that operating cash flow cannot absorb without disruption.

Key Person Life Insurance: The business owns the policy, pays the premiums, and receives the death benefit. The benefit replaces lost revenue, funds recruiting, and buys time to stabilize. Premiums are not deductible, but the death benefit is generally received income-tax-free. The annual life insurance premium is a fraction of the revenue at risk.

Key Person Disability: A key person disability can be as devastating as a death. When a key person cannot be in the office, the reason is not relevant to the bottom line. Key person disability coverage provides cash to the business during the disability period. The exposure it covers is more likely than death during working years.

The Owner as Key Person: In many businesses the most important key person is the owner. Key person insurance on the owner keeps the business running through the disruption. Buy-sell insurance, covered in Chapter 5, transfers ownership and protects the remaining owners. Both are needed. Neither replaces the other.

> **Reality Check**
> Most owners insure their own life twice over and never insure the one employee who controls more revenue than they do. That mistake stays invisible for years. It becomes visible exactly once: the day that person does not come back.

Big Mo

Big Mo owns a regional elevator service and sales firm with eight technicians and $3.8 million in annual revenue. His senior service manager, Garrett, runs the two largest property management accounts and accounts for $1.4 million in annual billings. Garrett has the relationships with the building owners, knows the quirks of every elevator on every account, and dispatches the technicians who do the work. Garrett keeps the business steady in an industry known for its ups and downs.

If Garrett does not show up on Monday morning, what happens to those two contracts and how does it impact the business?

Garrett is thirty-eight, healthy, and a non-smoker. A ten-year level term policy on his life with a $1.5 million death benefit costs $1,800 a year. The business owns the policy and is the beneficiary. The annual premium runs less than 0.2 percent of the billings at risk.

In year four, Garrett died in a car accident. The $1.5 million death benefit is paid income-tax-free. Big Mo hired a contract service manager at a premium rate to keep the service contracts on schedule, $140,000 over six months. He retained a recruiting firm to find a permanent replacement at $55,000 in fees plus a $20,000 signing bonus. Billings dropped 40 percent for two quarters during the transition, about $560,000 in lost revenue, leaving $725,000 in reserve. The business survived, with reduced revenue, short staff, and weaker client relationships through the recovery.

The policy is not an investment and it is not a product. It is infrastructure. The $1,800 annual premium positions $1.5 million of capital to arrive on the day the business needs it.

> **Rule Extracted**
> A key person policy that costs less than one percent of the revenue at risk is protection, not investment.

The Policy at a Glance

Key Person Policy Garrett	
Insured	Garrett, age 38, Senior Service Manager
Owner and beneficiary	The business
Death benefit	$1,500,000
Annual premium	$1,800 (not deductible)
Coverage	10-year level term
Revenue at risk	$1.4M in annual billings

Deployment of the $1,500,000 Death Benefit

Use of proceeds	Amount
Contract service manager (6 months)	$140,000
Recruiting firm and signing bonus	$75,000
Revenue shortfall coverage	$560,000
Remaining reserve	$725,000
Total death benefit	$1,500,000

Total premiums paid over four years: $7,200. The business absorbed a 40 percent revenue decline for two quarters and continued operations.

Business Overhead Expense Insurance

BOE insurance covers the fixed costs of the business during the owner's disability: rent, utilities, non-owner payroll, insurance premiums, loan payments, equipment leases. These costs do not stop when the owner cannot work. BOE insurance pays them so the business survives until the owner returns or a transition plan is executed.

Key person disability insurance replaces the revenue the owner generates and protects the income statement. BOE insurance covers the overhead and protects the balance sheet.

An owner needs both. Neither replaces the owner's personal disability income, which protects the household.

The BOE monthly benefit is sized to the monthly overhead. The premium is deductible. Benefits received are taxable, offset by the deductible expenses. Without BOE, the business must self-insure with cash reserves. A business with $50,000 per month in fixed costs needs $200,000 in reserves for a four-month lifeline. That capital sits idle instead of working in the business.

What This Means for You
Three coverages serve three different risks. Key person disability replaces revenue. BOE pays the overhead. Personal disability protects the household. None replaces the others.

Contingency Planning

Insurance covers the financial impact of a key person event. It does not cover the operational impact. The cushion provides time for the business to adjust. Contingency planning determines whether the business uses that time or wastes it.

Contingency planning operates on two timelines. The first seventy-two hours determine whether the business stabilizes or spirals. The weeks and months that follow determine whether the business can function without the missing person long enough to recover.

The 72-Hour Plan

The 72-hour plan is a written document that answers the questions no one can think clearly enough to answer during a crisis. Backup signatory authority. Banking contacts. Payroll processing. Top-twenty client communication protocol. Passwords and system access. Where every key document lives. Who steps in and what their scope of authority is.

For key employees, the plan is narrower: client contacts, project status, vendor relationships, system credentials, and the name of the person who picks up the work.

A 72-hour plan is not optional. It is the operational counterpart to the key person policy. It is as much for the spouse as it is for the business. The spouse should know the plan exists, where it lives, who to call first, what decisions can wait, and what decisions cannot. One step most owners skip: sit down with the spouse for one hour and walk through it together.

The 72-hour plan covers the first three days. The processes, contacts, and systems that carry the business past three days (billing, scheduling, vendor relationships, contract terms, renewal schedules) have to be documented separately and tested annually. A stale plan creates false confidence.

A key person event is a disruption, not a verdict. The business that planned for it continues.

Ask Your Advisor Today

1. Do I have key person life and disability coverage on anyone other than myself, sized to the revenue at risk?
2. Do I have BOE coverage sized to my actual monthly overhead?
3. Does a 72-hour plan exist, and has my spouse seen it?

Chapter 4: Retention Structures for Key People

Key people are always in demand. A raise is a cost the business pays without buying commitment. The alternative is a structure that makes leaving expensive and staying profitable.

> **Early Decision Rule**
> A raise buys twelve months of loyalty. A structure buys twenty years.

Deferred Compensation

The business sets aside a defined amount each year in a corporate account, the deferred compensation reserve. That account is a business asset, controlled by the business, not the employee. When the reserve is held inside corporate-owned life insurance or an annuity, it grows tax-deferred; held as ordinary investments, the corporation pays tax on its earnings each year. The contributions into the reserve are not tax deductible when made.

As the employee hits vesting milestones, the right to the benefit is earned. But earning the right and receiving the payment are two different events. The payout date is fixed in the agreement at the outset, typically retirement, separation, or a specified age. When the payment is made, the business takes the deduction, and the employee recognizes ordinary income. If the employee leaves before vesting, the business keeps the reserve. Section 409A governs these rules.

Russell and Betty

Russell owns Golden Anchor Insurance, a specialty yacht insurance brokerage with twelve employees and $4.2 million in annual revenue. Betty is the head of yacht accounts and manages the top forty clients. She handles renewals, manages claims, and knows every boat in her book by name. She earns $200,000 a year and her accounts generate $1.6 million in revenue.

Russell has been retaining Betty through salary increases since a competitor started recruiting her. He raised her to $230,000, then $250,000. Each raise bought temporary loyalty and nothing more.

> **Reality Check**
> A raise increases cost. It does not increase commitment.

Russell's alternative to the raise funds an asset the business owns and controls, builds loyalty the raise cannot buy, and costs less over twenty years than the salary increases already on the table.

The structure

The Indexed Universal Life policy (IUL) is not the retention product. It is the infrastructure on which the retention agreement is built.

The IUL on Betty's life has a $1.5 million death benefit. The business owns the policy, pays the premiums, and is the beneficiary. Over a long accumulation horizon, the cash value grows tax-deferred and compounds inside the policy without current tax on the gains.

Betty is a participant in a deferred compensation agreement that promises her beneficiaries a percentage of the death benefit if she dies during the vesting period and access to a percentage of the cash value when the vesting schedule is satisfied.

The business funds a flat $75,000 annual premium for ten years. Total premiums: $750,000. A $50,000 raise runs $1,000,000 in gross pay over twenty years, plus employer payroll tax, less the corporate deduction. On an after-tax, present-value basis the raise costs the business about $859,000. The structure costs

$750,000 and builds an asset the raise never creates, a difference of roughly $109,000 before counting the policy value. No premiums are paid after year ten.

The agreement includes a partnership provision. If Betty remains employed through year 20, she is admitted as a partner. The policy transfers as a tax-free partnership distribution. No compensation event. No ordinary income. The death benefit remains tax-free under the transfer-to-the-insured exception.

The numbers below reflect one design for Betty's situation. The premium, vesting schedule, and death benefit are sized to Russell's budget and Betty's role. Every element is adjustable. A smaller premium funds a smaller policy. A longer vesting schedule extends the retention window. The structure scales to the business, not the other way around.

Vesting Schedule

Year	Age	Vested	Transfer
5	45	50%	Taxable
10	50	75%	Taxable
15	55	100%	Taxable
20	**60**	**Partner**	**Tax-Free**

Policy Performance

$ in thousands. No premiums paid after year 10.

Year	Age	Annual Premium	Total Premiums	Surrender Value	Death Benefit
1	40	$75.0	$75.0	—	$1,500.0
5	45	$75.0	$375.0	$372.0	$1,500.0
10	50	$75.0	$750.0	$929.0	$1,827.0
15	55	—	$750.0	$1,270.0	$2,276.0
20	60	—	$750.0	$1,744.0	$2,866.0

Policy values are illustrative. They assume a 6 percent annual credited rate on an indexed universal life policy issued to a 40-year-old female at preferred non-tobacco rates. Actual values will differ based on the carrier, underwriting classification, credited rate, and cost of insurance. Non-guaranteed elements are not guaranteed and may be higher or lower than shown.

The business pays $750,000 over ten years and owns an asset worth more than twice that at year 20. At year 20 the surrender value is $1,744,000 and the death benefit is $2,866,000. In the raise scenario, that asset does not exist at all.

The table below shows what Betty keeps after tax at each vesting milestone. The values are lower than the policy performance table before year 20 because the transfer is taxable until the partnership provision applies. At year 20 the values match because the transfer is tax-free. The raise produces more take-home in the first five years. By year 15 the after-tax cash value exceeds the cumulative raise by $254,000. At year 20 the gap is $742,000 and the transfer carries no tax. The death benefit exceeds the cumulative raise from year 5 forward.

The Raise vs. The Structure

$ in thousands. All values after tax.

Year	Raise Take-Home	Vested CV After Tax	Vested DB After Tax	Transfer
5	$198.0	$139.0	$462.0	Taxable
10	$427.0	$520.0	$843.0	Taxable
15	$693.0	$947.0	$1,401.0	Taxable
20	**$1,002.0**	**$1,744.0**	**$2,866.0**	**Tax-Free**

> **Rule Extracted**
> The agreement creates a valuable asset. If Betty leaves, the business loses a key person but keeps the policy, which offsets part of the cost of replacing her. It is also more expensive for Betty to leave and more profitable for her to stay. The agreement creates that dynamic.

Russell and Betty: Golden Anchor Insurance

Outcome	What the business does	Result
Betty dies (during vesting)	Receives the death benefit tax-free; pays the vested percentage to her family as deductible compensation	Family protected; at year 5 the business nets over $1,000,000

Outcome	What the business does	Result
Betty walks (before year 20)	Keeps the policy; pays the vested cash value from operating cash (deductible); repurposes or surrenders it	Business protected; the asset is retained and the payout deducted
Betty stays (through year 20)	Policy transfers under the partnership provision (IRC §731); no compensation event, no ordinary income	Both win: Betty gets $1,744,000 cash value and a $2,866,000 death benefit, tax-free, and can keep it, annuitize under §1035, or take policy loans; the business spent $109,000 less than the raise

Other Retention Structures

Split-Dollar Life Insurance

Split-dollar is an arrangement between the business and the employee that splits the cost and benefit of a life insurance policy. Two regimes exist, endorsement and collateral assignment, differing in who owns the policy and how the business recovers its investment if the employee leaves. Chapter 8 covers the mechanics in full, where split-dollar is used for owner extraction rather than employee retention.

Phantom Equity

A key employee gets economic exposure to business growth without receiving actual ownership. The business defines a baseline value at the start and pays the employee a percentage of the increase in value at a future date. The payout terms, vesting schedule, and forfeiture conditions are set in the agreement. The employee recognizes ordinary income at payout. The business takes the deduction in the same year.

Restrictive Covenants

Non-compete and solicitation agreements make leaving costly by limiting where the departing employee can work and preventing them from taking clients or recruiting staff. Enforceability varies by state.

Design Choice Checkpoint
The right structure depends on what the business is paying for. Deferred compensation retains the asset if the employee leaves. Split-dollar pairs insurance need with ownership control. Phantom equity ties the payout to the performance the employee helped create. Restrictive covenants raise the cost of walking out the door.

The Russell and Betty case runs in a partnership, which enabled the tax-free transfer in year 20. That mechanic is not available to S-corp owners. The other structures in this chapter, deferred compensation, phantom equity, and restrictive covenants, work across all entity types. C-corp owners have additional extraction structures at the owner level that pair well with retention planning, covered in Chapter 8.

Retention is continuity from the front end. Done with a structure, it builds loyalty around an asset the business owns, instead of renting it year to year as a short-term expense. Chapter 5 covers the agreements that govern what happens when a partner dies, retires, divorces, or wants out.

Ask Your Advisor Today
1. For each key person I want to retain, is there a structure that makes leaving expensive and staying profitable?
2. If my top producer leaves tomorrow, what are the financial consequences for the employee and the firm?
3. Are my retention structures matched to each employee's role, the entity type, and the tax treatment of the eventual payout?

Chapter 5: Buy-Sell Agreements

A partner dies on a Tuesday. By Friday the estate owns a third of the company. The surviving partners want to keep operating. The family wants cash. Without an agreement that sets the price and the terms, both parties have a legitimate claim and no clean way to resolve it.

A buy-sell agreement is the structural backstop for ownership continuity. It is a contract between co-owners that dictates terms when a change in ownership occurs. A funded buy-sell executes on those terms. An unfunded one leaves the surviving partners scrambling for capital under time pressure.

> **Early Decision Rule**
> An unfunded buy-sell is a document, not a plan.

Trigger Events

Death: The surviving partners want to keep running the company. The family wants cash. Those goals are in direct conflict. Without an agreement, two people who both have a legitimate claim end up in court deciding which one loses. The buy-sell decides it in advance, on a day when everyone is still calm enough to be fair.

Disability: If a partner cannot work, the business dynamic changes. Ownership and distribution percentages have not. One fewer partner is running the business, generating revenue, and managing operations. The remaining partners absorb the workload at the same distribution split. That is not sustainable. A disability trigger resolves it. The disabled partner receives a predetermined buyout. The producing partners are compensated for their increased effort.

Divorce: When a partner divorces and a court awards the ex-spouse a portion of the business interest, the remaining partners are in business with someone they never chose. A divorce trigger gives the partners the right to purchase that interest at the agreed valuation.

Retirement or Voluntary Departure: A partner who wants out at 62 may trigger a buyout the business cannot fund on short notice. A retirement trigger built into the agreement creates the lead time to prepare for it.

Personal Bankruptcy. A creditor who seizes a partner's interest creates the same unwanted-partner problem as divorce.

> **Reality Check**
> Most agreements address death and skip the more likely triggers: disability, divorce, and personal bankruptcy. The triggers missing from the agreement are the ones that produce litigation.

Eric and the Davids

The structure of a buy-sell agreement determines more than who buys and at what price. It sets each surviving partner's tax basis, which determines how much of the eventual sale proceeds they keep after tax. Same business, same price, same transaction, a different structure produces a different outcome years later. The Eric and the Davids case shows how that gap is created.

Eric, his cousin David, and his other cousin David are equal partners in a maple syrup consulting firm in rural Vermont. The three partners cover production optimization, equipment selection, and sugarbush management. They have built the practice over fifteen years to serve operations from small family sugarbushes to the largest commercial producers in the state. The business is valued at $6 million. Each partner's interest is worth $2 million, and each partner's original basis is $500,000. The entity is taxed as a partnership.

Two types of buy-sell structures exist: cross-purchase and entity redemption. Both transfer ownership in full, but have different tax outcomes, administrative burdens, and update requirements.

Cross-Purchase

In a cross-purchase, each partner personally owns a life insurance policy on each of the other two partners. Three partners mean six policies each with a $1 million death benefit. When a partner dies, the two survivors each collect $1 million and use it to purchase the deceased partner's interest.

Cross-Purchase: Each Partner Insures the Others

Three partners, six policies. Every partner owns a $1M policy on each of the other two.

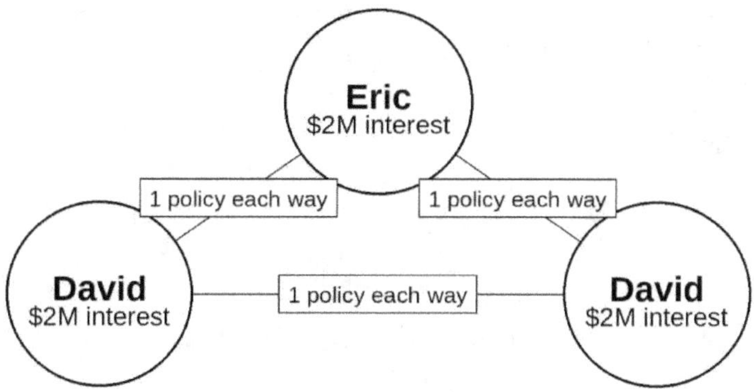

On a death, the two survivors collect $1M each and buy the deceased's $2M interest.

Survivors' basis steps up to $1.5M each.
Six policies to administer.

Each partner pays premiums with after-tax personal dollars. The premiums are not deductible. The death benefit is tax-free to the surviving partner who owns the policy. The surviving partners pay the deceased partner's estate with the policy proceeds. Code Section 1014 gives the estate a stepped-up basis to fair market value at the date of death. The estate receives $2 million ($1 million from each surviving partner). Each surviving partner now holds basis of $1 million in the portion purchased.

The surviving partners now each own $3 million of a $6 million business. Each surviving partner's basis has increased to $1.5 million: $500,000 for the original third plus $1 million for the portion purchased from the deceased partner's estate.

Entity Redemption

In an entity redemption, the partnership owns a policy on each partner. Each policy has a $2 million death benefit equal to the value of the partner's interest. When a partner dies, the entity collects the death benefit and uses it to redeem the deceased partner's interest. The estate receives the policy proceeds tax-free. The ownership percentages adjust without a separate purchase by the survivors.

Entity Redemption: The Business Insures Each Partner

Three partners, three policies. The entity owns one $2M policy on each partner.

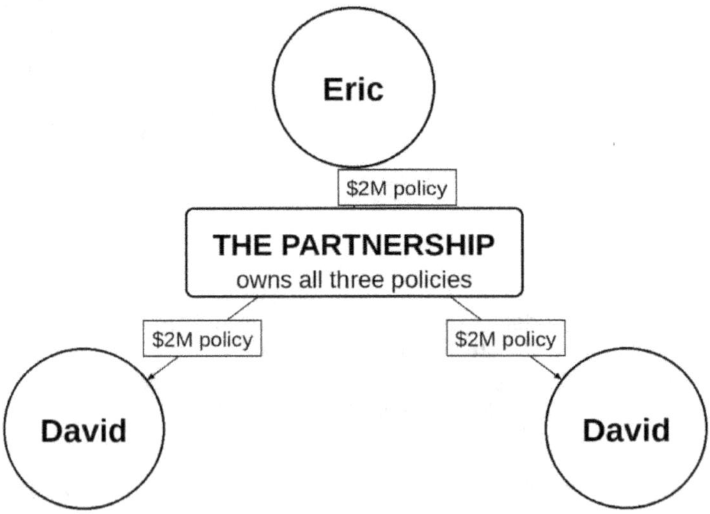

On a death, the entity collects $2M and redeems the deceased's interest.

No basis step-up; the original $500k basis stays.
One policy per partner.

The premiums are paid by the entity. In a partnership, premium payments are not deductible.

Each surviving partner now owns 50 percent of the partnership, worth $3 million, at the original $500,000 basis. The entity purchased the policy, so the surviving partners receive no step-up in basis on the redeemed share.

The Tax Difference
In both structures each surviving partner owns 50 percent of a $6 million partnership. The basis is different. Cross-purchase, funded with after-tax personal dollars, increases the survivor's basis and lowers capital gains tax on any eventual sale. Entity redemption uses partnership funds that were not deductible. The surviving partners receive no step-up in basis.

> **Rule Extracted**
> Cross-purchase preserves basis. Entity redemption does not. Same business, same buyout, different capital gains tax on the eventual sale.

The Coverage Gap

After the first death, each surviving partner's ownership interest has increased. The insurance coverage on the remaining partners has not. The agreement now covers less than the value of the next buyout. A coverage gap exists in either structure.

Cross-Purchase: Each partner owns a $1 million policy on the other surviving partner. The interest is now valued at $3 million. The shortfall is $2 million.

Entity Redemption: The partnership still owns a $2 million policy on each survivor. Each interest is now worth $3 million. The shortfall is $1 million.

Orphan Policies

In the cross-purchase, the deceased partner's estate owns policies on the surviving partners. The estate has no use for them. They have value: in-force death benefits at fixed premiums. Keeping them is cheaper than purchasing new coverage.

Code Section 101(a)(2)(B) provides an exception to the transfer-for-value rule for a transfer to a partner of the insured. The deceased partner's policy on one survivor can move to the other survivor, who is a partner of that insured, without the death benefit losing its income-tax-free status, provided the partnership is in force at the time of transfer. In plain terms: the surviving partners can take over the deceased partner's policies on each other without losing the income-tax-free status of the death benefit, as long as the partnership hasn't been dissolved. The transfers preserve the tax-free death benefit and narrow the cross-purchase coverage gap to roughly the entity redemption level. The basis advantage of cross-purchase remains.

The Tradeoff

Cross-purchase produces a better tax outcome. Entity redemption is operationally simpler. Three issues determine which fits the partnership.

Simplicity: A three-person cross-purchase needs six policies. Four partners need twelve. Entity redemption needs one policy per partner. The administrative burden scales fast with cross-purchase, and policy amounts must be recalculated any time ownership percentages change.

Affordability mismatch: In cross-purchase, each partner pays out of pocket for policies on the other partners. If one partner is older or has health issues, the younger partners carry expensive premiums. The same problem appears in unequal partnerships, where junior partners shoulder larger premiums on senior partners. In entity redemption the business absorbs the cost evenly.

Cash flow: The entity typically has more cash flow than any individual partner. Paying premiums from the business is easier even though it is not deductible.

A Note on Entity Types

Buy-sell agreements apply to every closely held business with multiple owners. The case above runs in a partnership, where the cross-purchase mechanics work cleanly. S-corp and C-corp shareholders face the transfer-for-value rule on cross-purchase policies. A transfer of a policy between co-shareholders is not covered by the partner-of-the-insured exception, so it can make a portion of the death benefit taxable. Entity redemption avoids the issue because the corporation owns each policy from inception and no transfer occurs.

Valuation of the Firm

The agreement names a valuation method. Common methods include an agreed fixed value between partners, a revenue or earnings multiple, or an independent third-party appraisal. The valuation should be reviewed every two to three years and the insurance coverage adjusted to match. A stale valuation creates a mechanism that was supposed to fund a clean transaction and now covers a fraction of the obligation.

Funding A Buy-Sell

Three funding sources exist for any buy-sell trigger: reserves, borrowing, and insurance. The right source depends on whether the trigger arrives with warning or without it.

For death and disability, the trigger arrives without warning and the buyout obligation is immediate. Insurance is the only source that produces capital the day it is needed. Reserves work only if they were built well in advance and sized to cover a sudden buyout, which most businesses cannot manage. Borrowing requires the surviving partners to take on debt under personal guarantee at the moment the business is absorbing a transition.

For retirement, divorce, and bankruptcy, the trigger has a runway the agreement can use. A planned retirement is funded by accumulated cash-value life insurance, reserves built from operating distributions, or a combination. A divorce or bankruptcy is funded through a structured payout from operating cash flow, a standby line of credit, or refinancing, matched to the timeline the court or the agreement controls.

The agreement should name the funding source for each trigger. Different triggers can use different sources.

> **Design Choice Checkpoint**
> The buy-sell is two decisions, not one. Structure determines the tax basis, the capital gains exposure at sale, and the administrative burden of maintaining coverage as ownership changes. Funding determines whether the agreement can be executed when a trigger occurs.

Disability Buyout Insurance

Disability buyout insurance provides the capital to purchase a disabled partner's interest after an elimination period of twelve to twenty-four months. Premiums are not deductible. Because the premiums are paid with after-tax dollars, the benefits are received income-tax-free. The waiting period is a feature. It confirms the disability is permanent before triggering an irreversible ownership change.

The most common mistake is funding the death trigger and leaving the disability trigger to operating cash flow. A business that relies on cash flow for a disability buyout is betting that revenues stay stable long enough to accumulate the capital. A partner disabled at 54 on a fifteen-year buyout obligation cannot wait for that capital to build. Disability buyout insurance converts that obligation into a fixed cost paid during the years the owner can afford it.

Ask Your Advisor Today

1. Is my buy-sell agreement funded for each trigger event: death, disability, divorce, retirement, and personal bankruptcy?
2. When was the valuation last updated, and does the insurance coverage match it?
3. Who has calculated the basis step-up difference between cross-purchase and entity redemption at my current ownership percentages?

ACT II CAPSTONE: Donald and Gil

Donald and Gil own Uncles Pharmacy and Soda Fountain, structured as a partnership. The painted sign in the window reads: "Filling Prescriptions and Glasses Since 1972." Donald is 60 and owns 65 percent. Gil is 40 and owns 35 percent. The buy-sell agreement sets a four-times-earnings multiple, valuing the business at $4 million today. Donald's interest is $2.6 million. The agreement includes a mandatory buyout when Donald reaches 75.

Gil projects that in fifteen years, net income will have doubled to $2 million, and the business will be worth $8 million. Donald's interest will be $5.2 million. Gil's current after-tax income is $265,000.

Gil has three tools to fund the buyout. The following analysis examines what each one produces for his household, his flexibility, and Donald's net proceeds.

Self-Funding
To accumulate $5.2 million over fifteen years earning 5 percent, Gil needs to reserve $241,000 per year. The pharmacy is a partnership. The annual interest on the reserve flows through the K-1 and is taxed at Gil's marginal rate. The net after-tax return on the reserve is closer to 3.25 percent. Gil needs to reserve $274,500 annually to meet Donald's payout, and that exceeds his take-home pay. Self-funding leaves Gil exposed to the buy-sell if Donald dies before 75.

Borrowing
At Donald's retirement, Gil arranges a $5.2 million business loan at 7 percent over ten years. The annual payment is $740,000. The interest deduction reduces Gil's taxable K-1 income, but the bank requires a personal guarantee, restricts additional debt and owner distributions, and constrains Gil's operational decisions

for a decade. If rates are higher when Donald retires, the math gets worse. Borrowing also leaves Donald's death uninsured before retirement. A separate term policy would be needed for the fifteen years before the planned buyout. Borrowing makes the buyout executable. It does not make it advantageous.

Insurance

The third tool is permanent life insurance. Under this path, Gil owns a policy on Donald's life and funds the premiums over fifteen years. At Donald's retirement, if the partnership structure remains in place, the policy transfers to him as a tax-free partnership distribution with no gain recognized to either partner.

The tax contrast with a cash buyout is significant. A cash payment of $5.2 million triggers capital gains tax at 23.8 percent. Treating Donald's basis as fully recovered, the tax is about $1.238 million, netting him $3.962 million. A policy transfer delivers an asset Donald accesses through tax-free loans, with a death benefit that passes to his family income-tax-free.

Donald and Gil agree that a cash value equal to 70 percent of Donald's projected interest is acceptable consideration. On a projected $5.2 million interest, the threshold is $3.64 million at year 15.

A policy with a $3.225 million initial death benefit at $180,000 per year projects to $3.725 million in cash value and $4.715 million in death benefit at year 15, assuming the policy performs as illustrated.

Why the Partnership Matters

The insurance path works here for the same reason it worked for Betty in Chapter 4. The business is a partnership, and the tax-free transfer mechanic is available. In an S-corp or C-corp, the policy transfer to a retiring owner is a taxable event, ordinary income without the partnership distribution treatment, and an additional layer of corporate tax in a C-corp. Same policy, same retirement, a different entity produces a different tax bill.

Comparison

	Cash Buyout	Insurance Transfer
Donald receives (gross)	$5.2 million	$3.725M cash value plus $4.715M death benefit
Donald's tax cost	$1.238 million capital gains	$0
Donald's net to family	$3.962 million	Cash value through tax-free loans plus death benefit
Gil's total cost	Self-funding $4.1M (unavailable) or borrowing with substantial constraints and exposures	$2.7 million in premiums over 15 years

The insurance path costs Gil less and delivers Donald more, because it converts a taxable buyout into a tax-free transfer.

The comparison table isolates each path on its own terms. Most real plans combine all three. The Realistic Path below shows what that looks like for Gil.

Funding for Death

The permanent policy provides a death benefit of $3.225 million from day one. That exceeds Donald's current $2.6 million interest. The coverage is embedded in the $180,000 annual premium Gil is already paying. If Gil were relying on self-funding or borrowing, he would need a separate term policy at $12,250 per year.

The Realistic Path

The $180,000 annual premium consumes 68 percent of Gil's after-tax income. A plan that is optimal on paper but unsustainable for the household is not practical.

An appropriate plan starts with a smaller permanent policy sized to carry the death contingency from day one and seed a portion of the tax-free transfer at retirement. That is the backbone. Gil layers reserves on top, scaled as the business grows and the buyout figure comes into focus. Borrowing capacity is the third layer, preserved as an option when the trigger arrives rather than committed today at a rate negotiated for 2040.

The three layers absorb what no plan made today can fully model. A plan built around a single tool is brittle. A plan built around a coordinated mix of insurance, cash, and credit absorbs the surprise the single tool cannot.

Integration Check: Closing Act II

1. Does my key person coverage on the highest-revenue employee match what would be lost if that person did not show up Monday?
2. Are my retention structures funded against the same employees the key person policies are written on, so the same person is not both the unsecured retention risk and the uncovered revenue risk?
3. Is my buy-sell agreement funded against the current valuation, with disability triggers and a coverage refresh schedule, and is the funding source matched to the trigger event?
4. If both Donald's retirement and Big Mo's loss of Garrett happened in the same year, does my plan have the cash and the documentation to absorb both?

ACT III: Benefit Extraction

Most of what the business produces moves to the owner through ordinary cash distribution. A smaller part can move through structures the tax code rewards. Retirement plans, group benefits, and executive bonus arrangements each convert a business deduction into something the owner keeps. Stacked together, they move more wealth to the personal balance sheet at lower tax cost than any single channel can deliver alone. The entity determines which of them are available and how efficiently each one works.

Chapter 6: Retirement Plans

A retirement plan is the one place the tax code lets an owner move business profit to the personal balance sheet before paying tax on it. Contributions go in deductible, grow without current tax, and are taxed only when distributed in retirement.

For an owner who is both participant and plan sponsor, the plan is also a design decision. The type of plan, the contribution structure, the matching formula, and the ability to stack multiple layers on top of each other determine how much of the business's profit ends up on the owner's balance sheet. A rank-and-file employee takes the plan as offered. The owner designs it.

> **Early Decision Rule**
> The plan that fits the workforce is rarely the plan that fits the owner.

The Foundation: 401(k)

The 401(k) is the base layer. The owner defers a portion of salary as an employee, up to the annual elective deferral limit set by the IRS, which lowers the current year's taxable income when made pre-tax. Total contributions to the account, including employer contributions and after-tax amounts, are capped each year at the annual additions limit, $72,000 in 2026. The IRS sets the cap. Reaching it is optional: an employer is not required to design a plan that allows contributions up to that limit.

The employee deferral is the common benefit across all 401(k)s. Whether to allow Roth contributions, employer matching, profit sharing, after-tax contributions, or in-plan Roth conversions is a design choice. The owner controls not just their own contributions but the design of the plan itself. This chapter works through those choices and their associated costs and tax consequences across entity types.

Roth Inside the Plan

Roth 401(k) deferrals go in after tax, grow tax-free, and come out tax-free. The decision turns on current bracket against expected retirement bracket. Two extensions sit on top: in-plan Roth conversions move pre-tax balances to Roth in a year the owner chooses, and the mega backdoor Roth uses after-tax contributions above the deferral limit, converted once inside the plan.

Profit Sharing: Second Layer

Profit sharing is a discretionary employer contribution separate from any match. It is not tied to employee performance and can vary year to year. The allocation method is where the owner's advantage is created. A pro-rata allocation gives every participant the same percentage of compensation, simple to administer and expensive in practice. A cross-tested allocation groups participants by objective criteria and directs a higher percentage to the owner group, provided the projected retirement benefits across groups pass IRS testing. A cross-tested plan can direct 80 to 90 percent of employer profit sharing to the owner.

Life Insurance Inside a Profit Sharing Plan
A profit sharing plan can own a life insurance policy on a participant. Premiums are funded by the plan's tax-deductible contributions, and the policy can be moved outside the estate during the owner's lifetime under standard ILIT mechanics. The structure converts pre-tax retirement dollars, the most tax-inefficient asset to leave to heirs, into a death benefit that passes income-tax-free and estate-tax-free. Chapter 11 walks the structure end to end. The profit sharing layer is not only a contribution vehicle. It is also a position from which estate value can be redirected.

The Qualified Plan Stack

Three layers build on each other. Each adds owner contribution capacity on top of the one below.

3 Cash Balance Layer $301,000
Defined-benefit layer. Actuary sets the annual contribution. Favors older owners with a short runway to retirement.

2 Profit Sharing Layer $46,500
Cross-tested allocation directs most of the employer contribution to the owner group.

1 401(k) Foundation $24,500
Owner deferral plus 3% safe-harbor contribution. The base every other layer builds on.

SEP-IRA (old plan)
$70,000
owner contribution

Full stack
$372,000
owner contribution

Cost per dollar of owner contribution
SEP: $3.00 → Full stack: $0.26

Cash Balance: Third Layer

A cash balance plan stacks on top of the 401(k) and profit sharing. It is a defined benefit plan that sets a target retirement benefit, with an actuary calculating the annual contribution needed to reach it. Contributions are deductible in the year funded. Older owners receive larger contributions because fewer years remain to fund the target. For an owner with high income and a short window to retirement, the required contribution can exceed $200,000 per year.

Qualified Plan Comparison

	Profit Sharing	Cash Balance	Full Stack (401k + Profit Sharing + Cash Balance)
2026 Max Owner	25% of W-2; to $72k combined	Actuary determines	$200k–$350k+ combined
Employer Cost	Minimum via testing	Minimum benefit for all eligible	Safe harbor + minimum DB benefit
Roth Option	Employer-only contribution	No	Yes on DC layers
Funding	Discretionary	Mandatory once installed	Mixed
Stacks With	401(k)	DC plans	All layers combined
Best For	Owners wanting more than deferral	Older owners, high stable income	Maximum extraction strategy

Dollar figures reflect 2026 limits. IRS adjusts annually for inflation.

The Contribution Base by Entity

For pass-through entities, contribution limits depend on the income type that funds them. Single-member LLCs and partnerships use total net income as the base. An S-corp's contribution base is W-2 salary only; pass-through income does not count. C-corps work the same way as S-corps for contribution-base purposes: W-2 compensation determines the owner's limit.

Plan Design and Compliance

Qualified plans run on three rules. Each exists for one reason: the plan is a tax-advantaged benefit, and the IRS conditions the advantage on the plan serving the full workforce, not just the owner.

Rule	What it does	What it costs the owner
Non-discrimination testing	Blocks a plan that benefits only highly compensated employees	Guaranteed contributions to non-owner employees
Vesting schedule	Recovers employer contributions when an employee leaves early	Plan administration
Controlled group rules	Pull a second entity into testing when the owner or family hold interests across businesses	Actuarial and compliance fees

An outside administrator and an actuary handle the paperwork, testing, and filings.

Dominique and the Qualified Plan

Dominique owns The Antique Boutique, a boutique antiques and estate-valuation firm with twenty researchers, catalogers, and authenticators on staff. Pre-contribution profit is $1.8 million, the owner's W-2 salary is $300,000, and non-owner W-2 payroll is $900,000. The firm has been on a SEP-IRA since inception. It was the right plan at three employees. It is the wrong plan at twenty.

The SEP forces a uniform employer contribution percentage across the workforce. To reach the $72,000 cap, Dominique contributes 24 percent of compensation. Therefore, every other employee gets the same 24 percent.

The SEP costs three dollars in employee contributions for every dollar it puts in Dominique's account. The full stack costs twenty-six cents.

Two Plan Designs Compared

	SEP-IRA	Full Stack
401(k) deferral and safe harbor	—	$24,500 deferral; 3% safe harbor on non-owner payroll
Cross-tested profit sharing	—	$46,500 to owner; 5% to non-owners
Cash balance	—	$301,000 to owner; actuarial minimum to non-owners
Allocation method	Uniform percentage	Tested on projected benefits
Owner contribution	$72,000	$372,000
Non-owner plan cost	$216,000	$95,000
Cost per dollar of owner contribution	**$3.00**	**$0.26**

Same payroll, same salary, opposite ratio. The full stack allows for a lower percentage profit sharing contribution and adds a cash balance layer on top.

The cash balance plan works in the older owner's favor when the workforce is younger. Non-discrimination testing is satisfied on projected retirement benefits, not on current contribution percentages. Employee contributions have more years to compound, so a smaller current contribution to younger employees projects to a benefit comparable to the owner's larger current contribution.

> **Rule Extracted**
> The SEP serves a business with five people. It penalizes the owner with twenty. The full stack reverses the ratio because the IRS measures fairness in projected benefits, not contribution percentages.

A life insurance policy inside the profit sharing layer is the bridge from the qualified plan to the estate plan. Chapter 11 picks up that structure. The next chapter turns from retirement plans to group benefits, where the same design discipline applies one layer up.

Ask Your Advisor Today

1. Am I capped at the 401(k) default, and what does a profit sharing or cash balance layer add over a twenty-year horizon?
2. Has my plan been evaluated for an in-plan life insurance allocation?
3. Who has run a controlled group analysis across all entities?

Chapter 7: Group Benefits and Carve-Outs

The retirement plan moves pre-tax dollars to the owner's balance sheet. Group benefits do something different. They use the business's employee pool to give the owner access to coverage and tax treatment that the individual market cannot match. The larger and younger the workforce, the better the terms.

> **Early Decision Rule**
> The business's employee pool is a planning asset. Most owners never use it.

The Employee Pool as a Planning Asset

Group benefits are the coverage a business offers its employees as a group: health, life, disability, and long-term care insurance. Bought individually, each of these is medically underwritten. The insurer examines the applicant's health, age, and history, then sets the price, limits the coverage, or declines it outright. An owner with a health condition can pay far more than a healthy one or be unable to buy the coverage at all.

Group coverage changes the basis of that decision. It is underwritten on the census, the workforce summarized by age, gender, salary, and job title, rather than on any one person's medical history. The carrier prices one rate for the group, and individual health is not a factor.

The tax advantage runs to W-2 employees. The premium is deductible to the business and excluded from the employee's income. C-corp owners qualify fully. Partners, sole proprietors, and more-than-2-percent S-corp shareholders do not receive the income exclusion, though they retain access to the group underwriting itself.

> **Reality Check**
> An owner who cannot buy coverage on their own can often get it through the business. The employees are the reason.

Defined Classes and Carve-Outs

Benefits do not have to be equal across the workforce. A carve-out provides enhanced coverage to a defined class, identified by salary threshold, job title, or job function. The class cannot name a specific person, but it can be structured so the owner is currently the only one who qualifies, as long as anyone who later meets the criteria would also be included.

Benefit	Class Required?	Notes
Section 79 Carve-Out	Yes	Class defined by salary, title, or job function. Actuary signs off. Requires 10+ employees for group plan.
Group Life/ Disability	All eligible employees	Carve-out tier within the group plan can be limited to a defined class.
Long-Term Care (C-corp)	No	No non-discrimination requirement. Owner only is permissible. Tiered contributions allowed.

Group Disability and the Carve-Out

Group disability insurance typically replaces 60 percent of salary up to a monthly cap, priced on the employer census with no individual health underwriting. That cap works for most employees. It does not replace 60 percent of an owner's income at $400,000 or $800,000. The carve-out layers a second policy on top for a defined executive class, lifting the cap, sharpening the definition to own-occupation, and paid for by the business.

Disability Coverage Summary

What each layer protects, how it is underwritten, and how the premium determines the tax treatment.

	Layer 1: Personal Disability	Layer 2: Group Disability Carve-Out
What It Protects	Household income	Income gap above individual policy cap
Typical Benefit	50–60% of personal income up to policy cap	Higher monthly cap. Own-occupation definition.
Underwriting	Individual. Full medical underwriting.	Group census. Guaranteed issue or simplified underwriting.
Uninsurable Owner	May be declined.	Covered through census. This may be the only income protection available.
Tax Treatment: Pre-Tax Premium	Benefit is taxable income at claim.	Benefit is taxable income at claim.
Tax Treatment: After-Tax Premium	Benefit is received tax-free.	Benefit is received tax-free.

Business overhead expense insurance (BOE) sits alongside this stack and covers fixed business costs rather than personal income. Chapter 3 covered BOE in detail.

> **What This Means for You**
> A working adult in their early forties is more than three times more likely to be disabled for 90 days or more than to die before age 65. A plan that addresses death and not disability is solving the less likely problem.
> Source: Social Security Administration, Disability and Death Probability Tables, 2023.

Disability coverage protects income. The next benefit protects something income cannot cover on its own.

Group Long-Term Care Insurance

Nearly 70 percent of adults who reach age 65 will need long-term care services, but roughly 30 percent of applicants between 50 and 65 are declined on the individual market. Group LTC closes that gap. Employers with 500 or more employees access true guaranteed-issue plans. Groups of ten or more access simplified underwriting that is far easier to pass than the individual market. Smaller businesses use multi-life plans that package individual policies at a group discount with standard underwriting.

Group LTC has no non-discrimination requirement. The business can cover the owner alone, a defined class, or any subset, with tiered contributions permitted. Spousal and family coverage can be added. The initial enrollment window offers the most favorable underwriting terms.

How LTC Premiums Are Taxed by Entity

The tax treatment differs sharply by entity. The C-corp deducts the full premium with no age cap and no income inclusion to the owner. Pass-through owners deduct only up to age-based limits that run from $500 at age 40 and under to $6,200 above age 70, with the excess not deductible.

LTC Tax Treatment by Entity

How entity type affects deductibility, income inclusion, and after-tax cost.

	C-corp	Pass-Through (S-corp, Partnership, Sole Prop)	Individual (No Entity)
Deductibility	Full premium. No age cap.	Self-employed health insurance deduction, up to age-based limits.	Itemized medical expense only above 7.5% of AGI. Most will not clear this.

Income Inclusion	None. Excluded from owner's income.	Wash above the age-based cap.	None (self-funded).
Example: Owner Age 55, $5,000 Premium	$5,000 deducted. After-tax cost: $3,950.	$1,860 deducted. After-tax cost: $4,312.	$0 deducted. After-tax cost: $5,000.
Example: Owner + Spouse. Both Age 55+, $10,000 Premium	$10,000 deducted. After-tax cost: $7,900.	$3,720 deducted. After-tax cost: $8,624.	$0 deducted. After-tax cost: $10,000
Benefit Received	Tax-free up to greater of actual expenses or the daily statutory limit.	Same.	Same.

Pass-through calculations assume 37 percent federal marginal rate. Age-based limits per Code Section 7702B for 2026

> **Rule Extracted**
> The C-corp deducts the full long-term care premium with no income inclusion to the owner. A pass-through owner deducts only up to an age-based cap. The entity determines the after-tax cost of the same coverage.

Long-term care protects against a late-life expense. The next structure, group life insurance, protects the family's balance sheet and funds an asset for the owner.

The Group Plan Path: Group Life Insurance and Section 79

Group term life insurance is governed by Code Section 79. The first $50,000 of coverage per employee is tax-free. Above $50,000, the employee reports a small annual charge set by an IRS table, for a 50-year-old, about $0.23 per $1,000 of coverage per month. A $1 million policy generates roughly $2,600 of reportable income a year.

The Section 79 carve-out uses that mechanic to fund a permanent policy for the owner. The structure works for a C-corp, where the corporation deducts the premium as a separate taxpayer and the owner takes none of it into income. The business pays the full premium as a deductible expense. The owner reports only the small Table I charge on coverage above $50,000, not the premium itself. A large permanent policy gets funded at a fraction of its actual cost to the owner.

The structure fits naturally with estate planning. When the policy is owned by an irrevocable trust, the death benefit passes outside the taxable estate. The annual gift to the trust is measured by the Table I charge, not the premium, so the policy is funded while consuming almost none of the annual gift exclusion. Chapter 11 covers the exclusion mechanics in full.

> **Design Choice Checkpoint**
> Section 79 requires ten or more employees and a definable class. For pass-through owners, who cannot use this structure, the Section 162 bonus in Chapter 8 produces a comparable result.

Dominique and the Group Plan Path: Section 79

Dominique's qualified plan from Chapter 6 is in place. The Antique Boutique is structured as a C-corp, and Dominique, age 50, is a super-preferred non-tobacco risk. He is married with two children.

Dominique wants a permanent policy owned by an irrevocable life insurance trust to provide estate liquidity for his family. The corporation commits $50,000 per year of net cost for ten years. The policy is designed as a maximum non-MEC, meaning the death benefit is set at the minimum required to keep the policy outside Modified Endowment Contract (MEC) status at the funding level. A policy that crosses into MEC status loses tax-free access to its cash value. Cash value accumulation is the primary objective.

How the Numbers Work

The corporation pays the full premium of $61,801 per year and deducts it. Dominique reports only the small Table I charge on coverage above $50,000, and the corporation adds a modest salary gross-up that covers even that. After the corporate deduction, the net cost to the company lands at $50,000 per year. Dominique funds the policy and pays nothing out of pocket.

The Policy Over Twenty Years

Premiums are paid for ten years. Cash value continues to grow on its own.

	Carve-Out ($61,801 Prem)
Cumulative premium paid (10 years)	$618,010
Initial death benefit	$966,538
Year 10 cash value	$748,240
Year 10 death benefit	$1,191,296
Year 20 cash value	**$1,401,977**
Year 20 death benefit	**$1,902,349**

Policy values are illustrative. They assume a 6.5 percent illustrated rate on a maximum non-MEC permanent policy issued to a 50-year-old male at super-preferred non-tobacco rates. Actual values will differ by carrier, credited rate, and cost of insurance. Non-guaranteed elements may be higher or lower than shown.

Cash Value and Death Benefit

Cash value inside a non-MEC policy is accessible through tax-free policy loans at any time without triggering a taxable event. At Dominique's death, the death benefit passes income-tax-free to the ILIT. Because the trust owns the policy from inception, the death benefit also passes outside his taxable estate. His spouse and children receive the proceeds without estate tax exposure on the insurance asset.

Chapter 8 turns to structures that work without the group plan. Three paths move corporate dollars into a permanent policy, each with a different tax profile and a different point at which the bill comes due.

Ask Your Advisor Today

1. What are my group's guaranteed-issue limits, and what would an executive carve-out add at each layer?
2. If I became disabled tomorrow, what is the dollar gap between my coverage and my actual personal income plus business overhead?
3. If I am a C-corp owner, is the business paying my long-term care premium and deducting it with no income inclusion?
4. Who has modeled a Section 79 carve-out at my current workforce size and confirmed I qualify for the group plan foundation it requires?

Chapter 8: Individual Extraction Structures for the Owner

Retirement plans have contribution limits and group carve-outs require an employee pool. The benefits to the owner are accompanied by the cost of including everyone else.

This chapter focuses on structures that move wealth to the owner alone. Without the employee pool, the owner pays more per dollar of coverage. Without the employee cost, the total outlay is lower. Every structure answers the same question: what is the most tax-efficient way to move a corporate dollar onto the owner's personal balance sheet.

Three extraction structures for a C-corp follow: a Section 162 bonus, split-dollar under the endorsement regime, and split-dollar under the collateral assignment regime. The capstone compares all three with the Group Plan Path with Section 79 carve out from Chapter 7, using dividend-and-invest as the baseline.

> **Early Decision Rule**
> The right structure moves the most value from the business to the owner.

The Structures in This Chapter

Structure	Who Owns the Policy	Owner's Annual Tax During Accumulation	The Tradeoff
Bonused (Section 162)	Owner from day one	Full bonus as W-2 income	Simplest structure. Most personal tax during accumulation.
Split-Dollar Endorsement	Corporation until cancellation	A small annual charge for the coverage	Low annual tax. At transfer the business relinquishes its claim,

			which is compensation income to the owner.
Split Dollar Collateral Assignment	Owner from day one	Imputed interest on the loan balance, which grows as the loans add up	The loan grows over time and is settled at transfer or death. If the business forgives it, that is compensation income to the owner.

The Baseline: Just Take a Dividend

Each structure carries a different tax profile, and the best one for a given owner depends on their current tax bracket, expected future tax bracket, and time horizon. The benchmark for all of them is the straightforward option: distribute the same dollars as a qualified dividend. This generates no corporate deduction and adds personal tax when received. The appeal of the structures in this chapter exists only if they offer a greater benefit than this baseline.

The Bonused Path: Section 162 Executive Bonus Plan

The corporation pays the owner a bonus, deducts it as compensation, and the owner reports it as wages and uses what is left to fund a permanent policy in their own name. The owner holds the policy from day one, with no vesting and nothing to unwind.

For Dominique, the bonus is grossed up so that after wage tax the remainder covers the premium and his out-of-pocket cost is zero. After the corporate deduction, the net cost lands at $50,000 a year, the same figure used for the Group Plan Path in Chapter 7. Over ten years the corporation lays out $500,000.

The full bonus is taxed as wages every year it is paid, making it the highest annual tax cost of any structure in this chapter. Placed inside an ILIT from inception, the death benefit passes estate-tax-free. The capstone shows what the structure produces in policy values against the alternatives.

The Corporate-Funded Path: Split-Dollar Under the Endorsement Regime

Chapter 4 introduced split-dollar as a retention tool, with the policy on a key employee. Here the insured is the owner, and the goal is to transfer corporate dollars into a personal policy at the lowest annual tax. The corporation funds the premium directly and keeps a contractual right to recover what it paid, so the owner is taxed each year only on a small coverage charge instead of the full premium. Written provisions govern who owns the policy, what the corporation recovers, when recovery is triggered, and how each step is taxed.

Take the endorsement version for Dominique, same case and same $50,000 of net corporate cost, now funding split-dollar instead of the bonus. For ten years the corporation pays the full premium directly to the carrier, about $49,000 a year. Dominique's only annual cost is the income tax on the small coverage charge. A modest salary gross-up covers the additional taxes, so his out-of-pocket cost is zero.

At year 10, the corporation cancels its recovery right, creating a taxable event for Dominique. The table below shows how the corporate deduction, a dividend, and a tax-free policy withdrawal cover the tax bill, resulting in no out of pocket expense.

Year-10 Cancellation: Cash Flow

Step	What Happens	Amount
1.	Corporation cancels recovery right on $491,000 in cumulative premiums	—
2.	Dominique reports $491,000 as ordinary income; owes $182,000 in tax	($182,000)
3.	Corporation deducts the same $491,000, saving $103,000 in corporate tax, and pays that $103,000 to Dominique as a qualified dividend	$103,000
4.	Dominique owes $24,514 tax on that distribution	($24,514)
5.	Dominique withdraws $103,514 from the policy's cash value, tax-free, to cover the rest	$103,514

Step	What Happens	Amount
Net personal outlay		$0

The year-10 tax bill is real, but it is paid entirely from dollars the structure already created, not from Dominique's pocket.

The Corporate-Funded Path: Split-Dollar Under the Collateral Assignment Regime

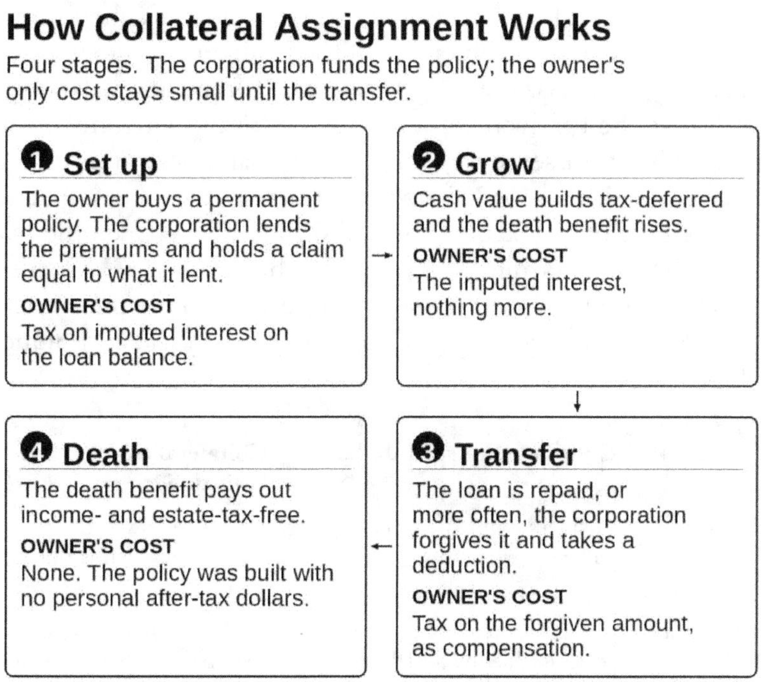

Collateral assignment split-dollar works in four steps: the business lends each year's premium to the owner; the owner's policy grows as a personal asset; the business tracks the cumulative loan as a receivable; and at transfer or death, the loan is settled and the remainder passes to the family.

During accumulation, Dominique's annual tax cost is the imputed interest on the growing loan balance, calculated at the applicable federal rate (AFR), the minimum interest rate the IRS publishes monthly for loans like this one. In year one, the loan is $49,118 and the imputed interest is small. By year ten, the cumulative loan balance reaches roughly $491,000, and the annual imputed interest has grown accordingly. Each year's charge is taxable income to Dominique, but the amounts remain modest relative to the endorsement path's year-10 cancellation event.

There is still a terminating event, and like the endorsement path it is generally taxable. At transfer the loan must be settled. The owner can repay it from personal funds, which triggers no tax but requires cash, or the corporation can forgive the balance, in which case the forgiven amount is compensation income to the owner. The endorsement path works the same way at its end: the corporation either recovers its premiums or gives them up, and only the give-up is taxable. The real difference between the two is not whether a terminal tax can occur but where the owner's annual cost comes from, imputed interest on a loan the owner holds, rather than a coverage charge on a policy the corporation holds.

	Endorsement split-dollar	**Collateral assignment split-dollar**
Ownership	Business owns the policy and pays the premiums	Employee owns the policy; the business lends the premiums
Annual tax to the employee	A small annual charge for the coverage, set by an IRS table	Imputed interest on the loan balance, which grows as the loans add up
At death or termination	Business recovers its cumulative premiums from the death benefit; the remainder goes to the family	Business recovers the cumulative loan balance from the death benefit or cash value; the remainder goes to the beneficiaries

	Endorsement split-dollar	Collateral assignment split-dollar
Cost at transfer to the owner	Business either recovers its premiums (no tax to the owner) or gives them up, in which case the rolled-out value is taxable as compensation	Business either recovers its loan (no tax to the owner) or forgives it, in which case the forgiven amount is taxable as compensation
Bottom line	Corporation owns it until transfer; the cost is recovered or given up	Owner owns it from day one; the cost is recovered or forgiven

These structures carry real advantages that depend on disciplined execution. A split-dollar agreement that drifts out of compliance with Section 409A, or a policy funded so aggressively it becomes a Modified Endowment Contract, converts an advantage into a problem. Annual review is not optional.

> **Rule Extracted**
> No structure transfers wealth to the owner's balance sheet entirely tax free. Taxes, ownership control, and loan forgiveness assumptions each affect the outcome. The structure that best fits the owner depends on how those factors weigh against each other given the owner's objectives.

Pass-Through and Partnership Owners

These structures are built for C-corp owners. The value for pass-through owners is a clean formalization, not tax savings. Two exceptions: partnerships can move a policy between partners tax-free using the Section 731 mechanic from the Donald and Gil capstone. And an S-corp owner who expects a lower bracket in retirement can use collateral assignment split-dollar, with the company forgiving the balance in a low-bracket year.

Ask Your Advisor Today

1. Which of these structures produces the best after-tax result for the coverage I need, and how does my entity type impact the decision?
2. If I am a C-corp owner, what is the difference in value between Section 162 bonus, the Section 79 carve-out, and split-dollar at the same net corporate cost?
3. If my C-corp carries large retained earnings, how much will a collateral assignment split-dollar policy convert into tax-efficient estate value?

ACT III CAPSTONE: Dominique's Options

Over the last three chapters, Dominique put the retirement plan stack in place, a 401(k), cross-tested profit sharing, and cash balance layer moving $372,000 a year onto his balance sheet. This capstone addresses the next layer: what to do with the remaining corporate dollars. The options are:

- Chapter 7: the Group Plan Path, a permanent life insurance policy funded through a Section 79 group term life carve-out
- Chapter 8: the Bonused Path, a permanent life insurance policy funded through a grossed-up W-2 bonus under Section 162
- Chapter 8: the Corporate-Funded Path, a permanent life insurance policy funded through a corporate premium advance under the endorsement regime
- The baseline: take the same dollars as a dividend and invest the after-tax proceeds

The first decision is whether an insurance strategy delivers greater value than a dividend distribution. The second is which insurance strategy best fits the owner's objectives.

The Comparison

Every path costs the company the same $50,000 a year for ten years. What differs is how much reaches the policy and what the owner pays in tax to get it there. The baseline is a dividend: the owner pays 23.8 percent (qualified dividend plus net investment income tax), leaving $38,100 to invest in a taxable account. The three insurance structures each deliver more to the asset: $39,873 under the Bonused Path, $61,801 under the Group Plan Path, and $49,118 under the Corporate-Funded Path.

The table shows the final result at year 20. The path to get there differs by structure: when the tax is paid, who owns the policy along the way, and what happens at the transfer. Those differences can make one structure more attractive than another even when the ending numbers are close.

The Three Structures at a Glance

	Annual tax during accumulation	Tax at settlement	Who owns the policy
Bonused Path	Full bonus taxed as wages each year	None; tax already paid	Owner, from day one
Corporate-Funded Path (endorsement)	Small insurance coverage charge each year	Compensation income if the business relinquishes its claim on the policy	Corporation, until specified transfer date (year 10)
Corporate-Funded Path (collateral)	Imputed interest each year on the premium loans	Compensation income if the business forgives the premium loans	Owner, from day one

The comparison that follows uses the endorsement structure for the Corporate-Funded Path. Collateral assignment reaches effectively the same year-20 values; in this example the financial difference between the two is negligible, and the difference between them is ownership, not return. Endorsement keeps the policy on the corporation's books until transfer, while collateral assignment puts it in the owner's hands from day one, which can help with creditor protection and estate timing.

	Dividend & Invest	Bonused Path (§162)	Group Plan Path (§79) Carve-Out	Corporate-Funded Path (Split-Dollar Endorsement)
Dollars to Asset	$38,100	$39,873	**$61,801**	$49,118
Annual Gift Tax	$38,100	$39,873	**$2,540**	~$1,800[1]

Exclusion Usage				
Dominique's Y10 Cost	$0	$0	$0	$103,138
Year 20 Cash Value	~$880,000	$902,828	**$1,401,977**	$903,759
Year 20 Death Benefit	N/A	$1,225,038	**$1,902,349**	$1,226,315

[1] Split-dollar uses the annual gift tax exclusion each year during accumulation (~$1,800) plus a large one-time gift at year 10 transfer equal to the policy's cash value at transfer (~$482,000 after Dominique's withdrawal). If the policy is owned by the trust from inception under a collateral assignment structure, only the annual gift applies. Dividend-and-invest cash value is the after-corporate-tax-and-dividend-tax residual ($38,100 per year) compounded at 8 percent for 20 years, before the brokerage account's eventual capital gains tax at sale.

What the Numbers Show

All three insurance structures deliver more value than a dividend distribution. The Bonused Path and the Corporate-Funded Path produce nearly identical year-20 outcomes. The Group Plan Path delivers significantly more cash value and death benefit than either.

The dividend column assumes the brokerage account is liquidated at year 20 with capital gains tax applied at that point. An owner who defers the sale would carry a higher pre-tax balance until realization.

Considerations Beyond the Dollars

The Group Plan Path with the Section 79 carve-out delivers the largest year-20 values but carries embedded costs and constraints the table does not reflect. For a business that already runs a group term life plan, the infrastructure cost is already being incurred and does not affect the comparison. For a business that does not, that cost must be weighed against the additional value before the Group Plan Path is the right choice.

The Bonused Path needs only a board resolution and is the easiest to unwind. Split-dollar requires a written agreement, ongoing tracking of the corporate recovery right, and a year-10 transfer that is not optional. The Group Plan Path carries the most administration and cannot be unwound without disrupting the group plan beneath it. The Bonused Path and Group Plan Path policies are owned by the owner from inception. Endorsement split-dollar is corporation-owned until the transfer.

The endorsement structure used here assumes the corporation relinquishes its claim at the year-10 transfer and distributes the corresponding tax savings to Dominique as a dividend to offset the resulting compensation income. Without those assumptions the owner's net position would be materially different.

From an estate planning perspective, the Group Plan Path and split-dollar each carry a small annual gift exclusion footprint, leaving most of Dominique's $76,000 annual capacity available for other trust funding. The Bonused Path consumes more than half that budget annually. Endorsement adds one large gift at the year-10 transfer. Collateral assignment, with the policy in the trust from inception, avoids that gift entirely and keeps the exclusion footprint small throughout.

These structures are built for the C-corp, where the corporation deducts the cost and the owner takes none of it into income. A pass-through owner does not get that treatment. A partnership can reach a similar result through the Section 731 transfer the Donald and Gil capstone used, and the Group Plan Path additionally requires ten or more employees in the eligible class.

For the C-corp owner who has already maximized the qualified plan, the question is no longer whether to move more wealth to the personal balance sheet, but which structure does it at the lowest tax cost. Act IV builds on these structures, using the same policies and accumulated wealth to fund the business exit and pass the estate to the next generation.

Rule Extracted
The right extraction structure depends on the business, the owner's tax position, and how the structure fits the estate plan.

Integration Check: Closing Act III

1. Have all four paths been modeled at the same net corporate cost on my actual coverage need: Section 79, Section 162, split-dollar, and dividend-and-invest?
2. Are my qualified plan, group carve-out, and individual extraction structures coordinated against the same annual gift exclusion, lifetime estate exemption, and W-2 compensation budget, or are they competing for the same capacity?
3. Is the wealth Act III is moving onto my personal balance sheet positioned correctly for the exit and estate decisions in Act IV?

ACT IV: Exit Strategy

Most owners think of the exit as a single transaction. In reality it is a multi-year process, and an efficient transfer depends on decisions made years before the sale. The same infrastructure that supports the transaction also strengthens the owner's balance sheet and protects estate value.

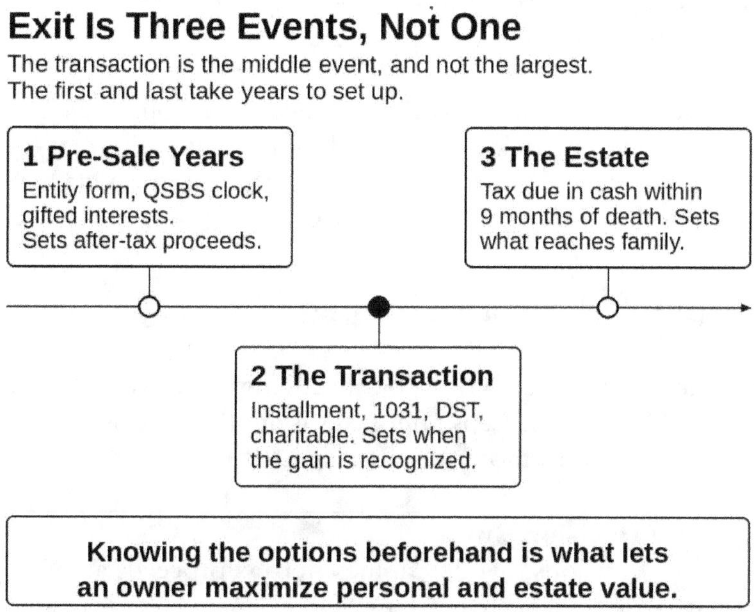

The pre-sale years offer the chance to put strategies in place that benefit the owner and the owner's beneficiaries. Structural choices about entity form, qualified small business stock eligibility, and gifted business interests should be addressed once a sale becomes a possibility, not once it becomes a plan. Planning for a sale is different from committing to one. The structures have to be in place well in advance.

The transaction determines the sale price and terms. The structure around it determines how and when the gain is recognized and whether the proceeds land inside or outside the estate. Lump sum, installment, charitable, 1031, deferred sales trust, and premium-financed insurance are options for controlling when the gain is taxed and how much the owner keeps.

The estate determines what reaches the family. Federal estate tax is due in cash within nine months of death. For an owner whose wealth is concentrated in enterprise value, real estate, or retirement accounts, that deadline is a liquidity problem. The demand for cash can force bad decisions.

The structures in this act work best in combination. Each has benefits and drawbacks, and the right mix applies different tools at different stages of the exit. The structures they provide have to be installed well before the exit arrives.

Chapter 9: Pre-Sale Planning

A higher selling price is one objective. How much of the proceeds the owner keeps after taxes is another. Decisions made in advance create a more tax-efficient transition.

> **Early Decision Rule**
> Many decisions that determine after-tax proceeds at exit are made three to five years before the buyer arrives, not at the closing table.

Section 1202: QSBS for C-Corp Owners

The clearest example is a tax break the owner either qualifies for years ahead of the sale or does not get at all. Section 1202 excludes the capital gain on qualified C-corp stock from both federal income tax and the net investment income tax. The One Big Beautiful Bill Act of 2025 (OBBBA) widened the exclusion and made the rules more generous and flexible than the version it replaced.

The exclusion is capped at the greater of $15 million or ten times what the owner paid for the stock, and it phases in with the holding period: half the gain at three years, three-quarters at four, all of it at five. The stock has to be C-corp stock, and the company's gross assets at formation cannot exceed $75 million. If those conditions are met after five years, a $15 million gain that would have cost $3.57 million at the top 23.8 percent tax rate disappears. Where the ten-times-basis cap lifts the ceiling above $15 million, the savings run higher still.

> **Reality Check**
> A C-corp formed before OBBBA in 2025 is governed by the previous legislation, whose terms were not as generous: $10 million exclusion, $50 million size test, no partial credit before five years.

The exclusion is built for active operating businesses: manufacturing, technology, distribution, retail, and most service businesses qualify, while professional services, financial services, hospitality, farming, and mineral extraction are not entitled to the benefit. When converting to a C corp, the five-year look back and the $75 million size test both start from the conversion date. A business that has already outgrown $75 million in assets no longer qualifies.

> **Design Choice Checkpoint**
> QSBS is one of three reasons a C-corp can outperform a pass-through, alongside the benefit deductions in Chapter 7 and the reinvestment math in Chapter 2. Any one can justify a conversion on its own. Weighed together, they often justify it by a wide margin.

Insurability Is the Planning Window That Closes First

Nearly every structure in this book runs on a life insurance contract, and every one of them assumes the insured can still qualify for coverage. That assumption expires. Age and a single health episode can take a favorable rating off the table, and once it is gone there is no structure to install. The window is widest when the owner is youngest and healthiest, which is usually years before a sale is even on the calendar. Premium financing, the structure that follows, is the clearest case for moving early: it funds a large death benefit outside the estate while consuming almost none of the lifetime gift exemption.

> **Reality Check**
> A tentative underwriting offer takes weeks and costs nothing. Preparing in advance creates the widest range of options.

Premium Financing

Like QSBS, premium financing is a pre-sale structure because it requires lead time. The policy must be issued and the loan must be in place before the sale, with enough runway to fund the policy and accumulate cash value through the transaction.

The ILIT owns the policy from inception, exactly as a standard ILIT would. What changes is who funds the premium. A third-party lender advances it each year, secured by the policy's cash value and death benefit, charging interest at a negotiated spread over a market reference rate. The grantor pays only that interest, and the interest is what counts as the annual gift to the trust. The premium itself never passes through the gift calculation.

The structure attaches to the owner rather than the entity and it works regardless of how the business is taxed. For a C-corp owner, it pairs with the QSBS exclusion from earlier in this chapter: the Section 1202 sale throws off tax-free proceeds, and those same proceeds retire the loan on a death benefit already sitting outside the estate. For a pass-through owner, it delivers the same estate liquidity without jeopardizing control of the business.

> **Reality Check**
> The annual gift in a premium-financed structure is the loan interest, not the premium. That distinction is the entire estate-planning case. Owners who fund the same coverage with personal premiums often consume ten times the annual exclusion capacity for the same death benefit.

Dempsey

Dempsey is 50. He built Butter's Better Biscuits, a premium dog treat brand, over the past decade. The product is sold in 2,400 independent pet stores and through the company's direct-to-consumer website, with regional distribution into specialty grocery chains. He expects to sell the company for $50 million within the next five years. The proceeds will combine with his existing wealth to produce an estate large enough that additional value will face federal estate tax at 40 percent on amounts above the exemption. He is married and in good health.

The Structure

Dempsey's ILIT applies for an IUL with a $10 million death benefit. The ILIT owns the policy from inception. It sits outside his taxable estate. Dempsey never owns it.

A third-party lender advances the ILIT $800,000 a year for the premium at 5.5 percent, with the interest capitalized into the balance rather than paid out of pocket. Dempsey and his wife make annual exclusion gifts of $38,000 to the trust, which applies them against the accruing interest. Over five years the loan balance climbs to about $4.5 million, and the couple has gifted about $190,000 in total, all of it within the annual exclusion.

The Exit

The company sells for $50 million, and after taxes Dempsey nets about $35 million. He repays the $4.5 million loan in full, leaving $30.5 million inside his taxable estate and a fully funded $10 million death benefit sitting outside it in the ILIT. The full accounting of what that cost and what it bought comes in the comparison below. The $190,000 in annual exclusion gifts moved a $10 million death benefit, projected to $27 million by life expectancy, beyond the reach of the estate tax.

The Loan Repayment Choice

Three paths satisfy the loan. Each moves the cost to a different place.

Path one: Dempsey repays the lender from sale proceeds. The IRS treats the payoff as a gift to the trust. The annual exclusion in the payoff year is applied first, and the remaining $4,424,000 consumes lifetime gift exemption. The policy is left unencumbered for the remaining 30 years.

Paths two and three keep the lifetime exemption intact. In path two, the trust borrows against the policy's cash value to retire the external loan, converting it to internal debt. In path three, the loan runs until death and the death benefit repays the lender first. Both reduce the death benefit available to heirs by approximately the same amount. Neither requires out-of-pocket payments, and neither consumes lifetime gift exemption.

The comparison below models path one, since it puts the entire lifetime-exemption cost into a single visible number rather than burying it inside the policy.

The Comparison

The right comparison is not the ILIT against the taxable estate. Dempsey has both in either scenario. The question is whether the ILIT exists alongside the estate. Below is the same family, same business sale, same growth assumptions. The only variable is whether premium-financed life insurance is in place.

Dempsey and Wife, Age 50 to 85	Do Nothing	ILIT Strategy
After-tax sale proceeds at age 55	$30,500,000	$30,500,000
Less: capital deployed to ILIT (five years of annual exclusion gifts)	$0	($190,000)
Net retained personal capital	$30,500,000	$30,310,000
Estate value at age 85 (5% annual growth, 30 years)	$131,819,000	$130,998,000
Less: federal estate exemption (2026, married couple)	($30,000,000)	($25,576,000)
Taxable estate	$101,819,000	$105,422,000
Federal estate tax at 40%	($40,728,000)	($42,169,000)
Net to heirs from estate	$91,091,000	$88,829,000
ILIT death benefit (outside estate, income-tax-free)	$0	$27,200,000
Total to heirs	**$91,091,000**	**$116,029,000**
Difference		**$24,938,000**

Estate values assume 5 percent annual growth from age 55 to age 85. Federal estate and gift tax exemption shown at the 2026 amount of $30,000,000 for a married couple. The ILIT Strategy column reflects $4,424,000 of lifetime exemption consumed at age 55 when Dempsey repays the loan from sale proceeds; remaining exemption is applied to the taxable estate at age 85. State tax not included and varies by jurisdiction.

What This Means for You
The policy did not beat the market. It moved wealth outside the estate before the tax was calculated. The estate tax is paid the same in both columns, with one adjustment: the ILIT strategy consumed $4,424,000 of lifetime exemption at the loan payoff, raising the estate tax bill by about $1,769,000. The cost is real. The benefit is the $27.2 million death benefit positioned outside the estate, delivered to heirs income-tax-free and estate-tax-free.
Same family. Same business. Comparable estate tax bills. One scenario adds $24.9 million to the heirs. The other does not.

When the Plan Does Not Cooperate

Premium financing is built around a planned liquidity event, and the plan does not always cooperate. The buyer never materializes, health or family or industry conditions shift, or the owner dies before the sale ever happens.

The structure does not collapse. If Dempsey dies in year three with a $2.55 million loan balance, the $10 million death benefit pays the lender first and the remaining $7.45 million passes to heirs through the trust, income-tax-free, with no estate inclusion. If the sale never happens, the trust can borrow against the policy's cash value to retire the third-party loan or let the structure run until death when the death benefit settles it. Both preserve lifetime exemption and reduce the death benefit available to heirs.

The structure was designed for the sale. It works without the sale. That is the difference between a transactional product and infrastructure.

The next chapter covers the structures that operate at the transaction: installment notes, 1031 exchanges, deferred sales trusts, and charitable lead trusts. Each address what happens to the proceeds rather than the business.

Ask Your Advisor Today

1. Do I qualify for QSBS? If not, is restructuring to a C-corp feasible, and when would the five-year clock start?
2. Has anyone modeled premium-financed life insurance against my estate exposure and confirmed the underlying insurability while I am healthy?
3. If we are three to five years from a sale, what should we be doing now that we cannot do later?

Chapter 10: Exit Structures: How Capital Changes Form

The structures in this chapter are installed at the transaction itself. None of them reduces the total statutory tax. What they change is the timing of recognition, who pays it, and where the proceeds land. They belong in a strong plan, but they are adjustments at the time of closing. They are not the foundation of a resilient infrastructure.

> **Early Decision Rule**
> The amount owed is only one variable. When it is paid, what is deducted against it, and who holds the asset when it is sold all change the owner's result as much as the rate does.

Installment Sales

An installment sale is the most common form of seller financing in private business transactions, with the buyer paying on an agreed schedule that usually runs three to ten years. It is common for a simple reason: most buyers of small and mid-sized businesses cannot put the full price in cash at closing. The seller's note bridges the gap and makes the deal possible.

Each payment has three components. The return of principal is untaxed, the prorated gain triggers capital gains tax in the year it is recognized, and the interest on the outstanding balance is taxed as ordinary income. Spreading the gain across years can help if the seller has stepped back from other income, since it leaves room to coordinate charitable gifts, retirement distributions, or Roth conversions into the same low-bracket years. The benefit is real but modest. An installment note is rarely a tax strategy. It is a deal-making mechanic.

The moment the note is signed, the seller becomes an unsecured creditor. This requires three things: a personal guarantee from the buyer, a security interest in the business assets, and a life insurance policy on the buyer sized to the outstanding balance. The rate is fixed at closing, so whatever the seller negotiates there is the only hedge against inflation for the life of the note.

Jeffrey and the Note

Jeffrey sells Irene Lane Cleaners, his commercial laundry business, to his plant manager for $4 million. The manager has $1 million in cash and no bank willing to finance the rest, so without seller paper there is no buyer at all. Jeffrey takes a $3 million note at 7 percent over ten years.

The note does two things a lump-sum sale would not. The interest throws off about $1.16 million in ordinary income across the term, and because Jeffrey has stopped drawing a salary, the gain he recognizes each year falls into lower brackets than a single year of full recognition ever could.

It also makes him a creditor for ten years. If the business falters under the new owner, the note is what is at risk. Jeffrey prices that risk into the deal: a lien on the equipment, a personal guarantee from the manager, and a $3 million term policy on the manager that declines as the balance pays down. He accepts the creditor position because the alternative is no sale at all.

> **Rule Extracted**
> The benefit of an installment sale is not tax savings. It is interest income on the outstanding balance, plus the bracket management on the gain, less the ordinary-income tax that the interest itself creates. The deal becomes possible when no other buyer financing exists. For a seller willing to carry the creditor's risk, the combination can add net value.

1031 Exchanges

A 1031 exchange defers the capital gains tax on investment real estate by rolling the entire proceeds into a replacement property, identified within 45 days and closed within 180. Every dollar has to be reinvested. Anything the seller keeps, whether cash or relief from debt, is taxable. If the owner holds the new property until death, the heirs inherit the asset at a stepped-up basis which erases the deferred tax liability.

A 1031 is a deferral tool, not a diversification tool. For owners who want cash or asset diversification, a 1031 delivers the opposite of what they need.

Deferred Sales Trusts

A Deferred Sales Trust, DST addresses situations where a 1031 exchange is unavailable or undesirable. The asset need not be real estate, no like-kind requirement applies, no fixed deadlines govern reinvestment, and proceeds can be diversified immediately by the trust.

Before a sale occurs, the owner transfers the asset to a properly structured DST, which sells it to the buyer. The seller receives a promissory note and recognizes gain only as repayments are received, spreading tax recognition across multiple years, often into lower-income or retirement periods.

DSTs require precise legal drafting, independent trustees, and careful coordination with tax counsel. Improper execution can collapse the structure and accelerate taxation. DST strategies must comply strictly with IRS regulations. They are generally appropriate only for larger transactions where flexibility and tax timing materially outweigh the complexity involved.

1031 Exchange Versus Deferred Sales Trust

	1031 Exchange	Deferred Sales Trust
Eligible asset	Real estate investments only	Investments, real estate, businesses
Replacement asset	Like-kind real estate	Any income-producing investment
Timing constraint	45 days to identify, 180 days to close	No deadline
Result	Stay in real estate	Exit to a diversified portfolio

Charitable Lead Trusts

A Charitable Lead Trust, CLT, fits an owner with three things at once: a charitable intent, an estate large enough to face the estate tax, and an asset that has appreciated. On its face those goals pull against each other, since every dollar given to charity is a dollar that leaves the estate and the heirs. The CLT is the structure that lets an owner serve all three at the same time.

It works in three steps. The owner puts an appreciated asset into the trust and takes an income tax deduction up front. For a set term, usually ten to twenty years, the trust pays a fixed amount to charity each year. At the end of the term, whatever is left passes to the heirs free of additional transfer tax.

The upfront deduction equals the present value of all the future charitable payments, discounted at the IRS Section 7520 rate. A stream of $250,000 a year for 20 years, discounted at the applicable rate, produces a deduction of roughly $3.12 million.

The deduction comes with a catch. The owner takes the full deduction now, but for the rest of the term the trust's investment income is taxed back to the owner year by year. That swap, a deduction today against the tax on tomorrow's income, is the mechanism the structure is based on. The asset is locked in for the full term, and the charity is paid every year whether the asset performs or not.

Shalom and the Appreciated Asset

Shalom owns a business worth $5 million against a $1 million basis. He has already used his federal estate exemption on earlier planning, so this $5 million is fully exposed to the estate tax at his death. He wants to support a cause he believes in and still leave as much as he can to his children.

Without the CLT, Shalom sells today, pays $952,000 in capital gains tax, and is left with $4,048,000. Invested at 5 percent for 20 years, it grows to about $10,740,000. The heirs receive $6,444,000 after the 40 percent federal estate tax of $4,296,000. Net to charity: zero.

With a grantor CLT, Shalom transfers the asset to the trust before selling. The trust pays charity $250,000 per year for 20 years. Shalom receives an immediate income tax deduction of about $3.12 million, saving $1,246,000 in Year 1 income tax. After the 20-year term, the remaining $5 million in the trust passes to his heirs free of estate and income tax.

The size of the deduction is set by the IRS, not by Shalom. It equals the present value of the 20-year charitable payment stream, discounted at the Section 7520 rate published for the month the trust is funded. At a 5 percent rate, that present value is about $3.12 million. The rate is fixed once the trust is funded, so the timing of the funding month matters.

The structure carries a cost the upfront numbers do not show. Because this is a grantor trust, Shalom is taxed personally on the trust's investment income every year of the term. The trust pays charity a fixed $250,000 a year regardless of what it earns. In this example the trust also earns about $250,000 a year, so the payment consumes the income and Shalom owes the tax on it, roughly $100,000 a year, out of his own pocket. Over 20 years, the future value of those payments is about $3.3 million. That money leaves his taxable estate, which reduces his estate tax, but it requires him to have the liquidity to fund the tax each year.

The Comparison

Shalom: $5M Position, $1M Basis	Do Nothing	Grantor CLT
Capital gains tax at sale	$952,000 paid	Avoided inside trust
PV: net capital after tax (today)	$4,048,000	—
PV: upfront income tax saving (today)	$0	$1,246,221
FV of net capital, year 20 (5%)	$10,740,549	—
FV of upfront saving, year 20 (pre-estate-tax)	—	$3,306,595
FV of grantor income tax paid ($100k/yr)	—	($3,306,595)
Net estate effect after 40% estate tax	($4,296,220)	$0
Trust remainder to heirs (estate- and income-tax-free)	N/A	$5,000,000
Net to heirs (FV at year 20)	**$6,444,329**	**$5,000,000**
To charity, PV today	$0	$3,115,553
To charity (FV at year 20)	**$0**	**$8,266,489**
Difference to heirs		**$1,444,329 less**

All figures are future values at year 20, assuming 5 percent annual growth. Capital gains 23.8 percent, federal estate tax 40 percent, income tax 40 percent (37 percent federal plus 3.8 percent net investment income tax). The grantor pays income tax on the trust's annual earnings personally, which reduces his taxable estate; that effect is shown in the net estate line. State and local tax not included and vary by jurisdiction.

The upfront deduction and the annual grantor tax offset exactly here because the example discounts the deduction and grows the assets at the same 5 percent rate. In practice the two rates differ, and the net effect tilts slightly toward the heirs when the funding rate is below the growth rate, or against them when it is above.

This example assumes the trust earns exactly 5 percent a year, the same as both the charitable payout rate and the Section 7520 rate used for the deduction. Under that assumption the trust principal stays at about $5 million for the full term, and that $5 million is what passes to the heirs. The principal holds steady only because the return matches the payout. If the trust earns more than 5 percent, the principal grows and the heirs receive more. At a 7 percent return, the remainder would be about $9.1 million. If it earns less, the principal shrinks. At 3 percent, the remainder would be about $2.3 million. The trust pays charity its fixed $250,000 each year regardless, so the investment risk falls entirely on the heirs' share.

Compared with retaining the entire asset for family wealth, Shalom intentionally redirects approximately $1.44 million of his heirs' potential inheritance toward charity, both measured at year 20. The heirs are not losing money to inefficiency. Shalom is redirecting it to charity by choice, and the full $5 million trust principal still passes to them free of estate and income tax.

What This Means for You
More than five dollars reaches charity for every dollar of reduced inheritance. For an owner with genuine charitable intent and estate exposure, that leverage is the appeal.

Design Choice Checkpoint
Installment notes make deals close. A 1031 exchange keeps real estate intact. A DST defers gains into lower-income years. A CLT pairs charitable intent with estate exposure. The right structure follows from what the owner wants to do with the proceeds.

The business has been converted into capital. What happens to that capital at the owner's death depends entirely on structures installed years before the sale was ever signed. Those are the subject of the chapters that follow.

Ask Your Advisor Today

1. If a buyer requires seller financing, how should the installment terms be negotiated, and what bracket management is available across the payment years?
2. If real estate is part of the business or the building, has 1031 versus DST been compared based on whether I want to stay in real estate or diversify?
3. Has anyone evaluated a CLT funded with pre-sale business interests at a discounted valuation, including the annual grantor tax and the liquidity it requires?
4. Which structures need lead time, and what is the timeline to install them before a buyer is at the table?

Chapter 11: Estate Planning for Business Owners: Liquidity, Equalization, and Control

The earlier chapters moved value off the business and onto the owner's personal balance sheet during life. This one goes a step further, moving it off the personal balance sheet and outside the taxable estate entirely. The work has to be done in advance, and the earlier it starts, the more it saves the people who inherit. Everything here is about the tax that comes due after the owner dies, and how much of it the beneficiaries are made to pay.

Irrevocable Trusts

Assets in the owner's name at death are in the taxable estate, including all future appreciation. A business interest worth $5 million today that grows to $15 million is a $15 million asset taxed at 40 percent.

The irrevocable trust changes this. The grantor transfers the asset to a trust for named beneficiaries, consuming lifetime gift exemption at the value on the date of transfer. From that point forward, all the appreciation happens outside the estate. The same $5 million business interest, transferred today, uses $5 million of exemption. If it grows to $15 million, the estate tax on that $10 million of growth never comes due. The asset was moved before it grew instead of after.

The cost is control. Once assets go into an irrevocable trust, they cannot come back out. In exchange there is a quieter advantage: the grantor pays the income tax on the trust's earnings personally, and the law does not treat those payments as additional gifts. Every dollar of tax the grantor covers is a dollar that stays inside the trust, compounding untouched for the beneficiaries. It is also a dollar that is removed from the estate before estate taxes reduce it. Moving a business interest in this way takes care, since it has to respect S-corp eligibility, partnership transfer mechanics, and the buy-sell agreement already in place.

Two gift resources fund the structures in this chapter, and most of them draw on the first. The annual gift exclusion is $19,000 per donor, per beneficiary in 2026, and it does not touch the lifetime exemption. For an ILIT with three Crummey beneficiaries, a married couple can move $114,000 into the trust every year without filing a gift tax return, which is enough to carry the premium on most insurance structures that follow.

The lifetime exemption is the larger reserve: $15 million per individual, $30 million per married couple. It covers the transfers the annual exclusion cannot reach, such as business interests, real estate, or a policy whose value runs past what annual gifts can fund. So a standard ILIT lives inside the annual exclusion, while a larger policy uses the premium-financed ILIT from Chapter 9, where the annual gift is the loan interest rather than the premium itself.

Val's Liquidity Problem and Life Insurance

Val owns The Crab Canoe, a chain of casual seafood franchises along the mid-Atlantic coast. By the projected death of the second spouse, she and her husband expect a combined estate of about $40 million: $28 million in the franchise company, $10 million in real estate, and $2 million in retirement accounts. The federal estate tax on the roughly $10 million above the married exemption comes to about $4 million, due in cash within nine months. The estate cannot raise it cleanly. Tapping the retirement accounts triggers income tax, and selling franchise interests or real estate against a deadline brings less than fair value. The estate is asset-rich, cash-poor, and liquidity challenged.

A permanent life insurance policy owned by an ILIT, sized to the estate tax exposure is a cost effective option. For married owners, a survivorship policy pays at the second death, as insuring two lives is less costly than one. The trustee uses the proceeds to provide liquidity to the estate.

The heirs inherit a working enterprise instead of the wreckage of a forced sale. The structure is not free: the premiums are a permanent commitment, the insured has to qualify through underwriting, and for an estate below the exemption there is nothing here to solve.

> **Reality Check**
> A portfolio cannot guarantee a specific dollar amount on a specific date. An insurance contract can, which is what the fixed estate tax deadline requires.

Repositioning Pre-Tax Retirement Assets

Pre-tax retirement dollars are the most tax-inefficient asset in an estate. They are taxed twice over: as ordinary income to the heirs when distributed, and as part of the taxable estate at death. A life insurance policy bought inside a profit sharing plan, then distributed out and moved to an ILIT, turns that worst asset into one of the best. Chapter 6 introduced the profit sharing layer as a place value could later be redirected from. Lewis is what the redirection looks like in practice.

Lewis

Lewis is 52. He owns Kupperbunds, a designer cummerbund and formalwear firm structured as an S-corp, selling through bespoke tailors and high-end retailers across the Northeast. The business is worth $6,000,000 today, and his profit sharing plan holds $3,000,000.

Lewis is married with three children. He forecasts that at age 80 the business will grow at 5 percent annually to $23,520,775 and the plan at 8 percent annually to $25,881,319. Together the estate will be worth $49,402,094, nearly $19.4 million over the current estate tax exemption for a married couple.

The profit sharing plan is a tax-inefficient asset in an estate. It is taxed twice: once as ordinary income to the heirs when they withdraw it, and again at 40 percent estate tax on the amount above the exemption. With no advance planning, the estate tax will be $7,760,838 and the income tax on the plan another $9,576,088. The $49,402,094 estate leaves the heirs $32,065,168. More than $17 million goes to two different taxes that fall on the same dollars.

Life Insurance through a Profit Sharing Plan

A profit sharing plan, unlike a standard 401k, can own life insurance, and the benefit reaches beyond the death benefit itself. It moves wealth outside the estate at a reduced value, and it turns an asset that would be taxed twice inside the estate into one taxed nowhere outside it.

Lewis realizes that moving his entire plan into a policy isn't realistic, since it will be needed for retirement spending. He deploys $100,000 a year for nine years from the plan to buy a survivorship universal life policy with a $5,000,000 death benefit. Lewis purchases a survivorship policy because it pays at the second death and a policy on two lives buys a larger death benefit than one on a single life. This strategy carries a small annual cost: the value of the insurance coverage is taxed as income each year, totaling $15,000 across the nine funding years.

At age 61, Lewis moves the policy out of the profit sharing plan into his own name. This is a taxable withdrawal, measured at cash surrender value less the economic benefit already reported. Even though $900,000 of premium was paid, the policy's cash surrender value is only $800,000, because policy expenses are front-loaded into the early years. The timing is deliberate. The taxable event is $800,000 minus $15,000, or $785,000 of ordinary income, taxed at 37 percent for a tax bill of $290,450. Lewis took control of his tax situation by choosing when and at what rate he pays the taxes.

He then transfers the policy to an ILIT, where the gift is measured at the $800,000 fair market value rather than the $5,000,000 death benefit it carries. With three children and gift-splitting, $114,000 falls inside the annual exclusion. The remaining $686,000 draws on lifetime gift exemption, which lowers the lifetime exemption at death from $30,000,000 to $29,314,000. A three-year survival rule applies: Lewis must live to age 64 for the death benefit to remain outside the estate.

The Whole Estate, Both Ways

The effect of the strategy is displayed below at Lewis' age 80.

	Do Nothing	With the Policy
Business value	$23,520,775	$23,520,775
Profit sharing plan value in estate	$25,881,319	$20,492,063
Tax paid at 61, value at age 80	$0	($1,253,495)
Gross taxable estate	$49,402,094	$42,759,343
Exemption remaining at death	$30,000,000	$29,314,000
Amount exposed to estate tax	$19,402,094	$13,445,343
Estate tax at 40%	($7,760,838)	($5,378,137)
Income tax to heirs on plan at 37%	($9,576,088)	($7,582,063)
Death benefit (outside estate)	$0	$5,000,000
Net to heirs after all taxes	**$32,065,168**	**$34,799,142**

Business at 5 percent, plan at 8 percent, age 52 to the second death at 80. The $686,000 of lifetime exemption used at the transfer lowers the exemption remaining at death, shown on its own line. The $290,450 income tax paid at age 61 is shown at its age-80 value, reflecting the growth those dollars would have earned in the estate. Federal tax only, state and local tax not included.

The life insurance strategy reduced the amount in the profit sharing plan and the total estate value, which lowered the tax liability. It also created tax free funds through a death benefit outside of the estate. The heirs keep $2,733,974 more, 8.5% more value, and the gain comes from infrastructure rather than investment return.

If the Second Death Comes Sooner

The estate tax depends on how large the estate has grown. The death benefit does not. If the second death comes at 70, the estate is only $26,427,774, below the exemption, and neither path owes estate tax. The $5,000,000 still pays in full, and the heirs are $2,846,740 better off. Lewis is not betting on when he dies or how large the estate becomes. The advantage holds either way.

The death benefit is not the only thing Lewis gained. Once the policy is his, its cash value is a source he can borrow against tax-free, for a business opportunity, a buyout, or income in a lean year, while the death benefit stays intact for the estate. The dollars he moved out of the plan were repositioned, not surrendered.

The Result
Lewis paid tax once, at a known rate, in a year he chose. That one event moved $900,000 of plan dollars into a $5,000,000 survivorship benefit beyond the reach of both taxes and left his heirs roughly $2,800,000 better off whether the second death came at 70 or 80. The lesson is not that insurance beats investing. It is that a pre-tax dollar left in the plan is taxed twice, and the only time to act is while the lead time still exists.

Estate Equalization

The next estate problem is not about tax efficiency. It is about whether the business survives an inheritance divided among children.

Lynn, Starr, and Hope

Lynn is a successful attorney who built her law practice from the ground up. Her daughter Starr joined the practice and became integral to its leadership. Her other daughter, Hope, has no interest in the legal profession.

The law firm represents most of Lynn's wealth, and Starr is the natural successor. Forcing a sale or splitting ownership would jeopardize both the firm's value and its operations. Starr should inherit the practice. The question is how to treat Hope fairly against it.

Lynn's estate is $6.5 million: a $4 million law practice, a $1 million home, a $750,000 portfolio, and $750,000 in retirement accounts. The obvious plan is to leave Hope all $2.5 million of the non-practice assets. However, Lynn will spend from the portfolio and the retirement accounts during her own retirement. By the time Hope inherits, these assets will be smaller, and the retirement portion is taxed as she draws it. The imbalance grows over time.

Lynn purchases a $3 million life insurance policy with Hope as the beneficiary. The amount is set to an estimate of the future gap between the practice and the non-practice assets. The tax-free death benefit replaces what income tax and Lynn's own spending take out of the non-practice assets, getting Hope back to rough parity with Starr in post-tax terms. The premium for a 60-year-old woman in standard health is about $30,000 a year, or $600,000 over 20 years.

At Lynn's death, Hope receives $3 million in cash, income-tax-free, on top of whatever non-practice assets remain. Starr receives the $4 million practice intact. Neither sister has to negotiate with the other, sell anything, or feel cheated.

> **Rule Extracted**
> The cost of equalizing was $600,000 in premiums. The cost of not equalizing was a forced sale of the firm or a fight between two sisters. The case rests on the family and the business, not the premium-to-benefit ratio. Lynn chose the premiums.

Generation-Skipping Transfers

Wealth passing from grandparent to child to grandchild is taxed at 40 percent at each generation. A GST-exempt trust shelters the assets placed in it, and their future growth, from that tax as they pass down through the generations. The structure fits estates large enough to support multi-generational planning. Above $30 million per spouse, dedicated GST planning warrants a separate conversation with the estate attorney.

Special Needs Planning

For families with a dependent who has a physical, cognitive, or developmental disability, a direct inheritance can disqualify the dependent from means-tested government benefits. A special needs trust holds assets for the dependent's benefit without being counted toward eligibility. Distributions supplement rather than replace government benefits.

The drafting requirements are exacting and state-specific. A special needs trust that inadvertently disqualifies the beneficiary from Medicaid or SSI has done more harm than good. If a dependent with a disability is part of the family, this structure belongs in the estate attorney's first conversation, not the last.

> **What This Means for You**
> An estate plan does not work in isolation. Every structure in this chapter rested on a decision made earlier somewhere else in the business: a plan funded years before, a practice kept whole, liquidity arranged before it was needed. Coordinate those decisions and the plan holds. Leave them disconnected and it does not.

Act IV closes with Solomon. One structure, installed thirty-four years before his death, provided the infrastructure for the buy-sell, the business liquidity, the Roth conversion, the partner buyout, and the estate tax at the end. The capstone shows what coordination looks like when it works.

Ask Your Advisor Today

1. What is my estate tax exposure, and where does the cash come from within nine months?
2. Do I need life insurance to pay estate tax, to equalize heirs, or both, and is each policy sized and owned correctly for its job?
3. If the business passes to one child, what is the equalization plan and is it funded?
4. Does my heirs' inheritance arrive in a form they can use, or does it require them to sell, borrow, or negotiate to access it?

ACT IV CAPSTONE: Solomon, One Policy, Five Functions

This capstone reaches beyond Act IV. It draws on structures from across the book, the ones that built and protected Solomon's business and personal balance sheet over 34 years. The infrastructure went in at age 48, and it adapted to whatever risk or opportunity arrived first.

Solomon owned a plumbing supply distribution company with 60 employees, three warehouses, $18 million in annual revenue, and $2 million in owner income. He held 65 percent. His partner Jack held 35 percent, which put Jack's share of the income at roughly $700,000 a year. The business was valued at $14 million when the policy was placed, making Solomon's interest worth about $9 million and Jack's about $5 million.

Jack owned a permanent cash-value policy on Solomon's life, a $5 million death benefit at an $85,000 annual premium. As partners, they could move the policy between them without the death benefit ever losing its income-tax-free status, a flexibility that would matter more than once over the years ahead.

The premium secured one obligation, the buyout at Solomon's death, but that was the smallest part of what the contract could do. Its real value was flexibility. The same policy would serve a different purpose depending on which need arrived first, and over 34 years it served five. When it was placed, no one knew which function would be called on first, or what the death benefit would be worth when it came. What follows are five separate calls the same policy could answer. They did not all happen, and they did not happen in order. Each shows the one structure meeting a different need. One policy. Five functions. Thirty-four years.

Function One: Buy-Sell Funding at an Early Death
Had Solomon died before retirement, the buy-sell agreement required Jack to acquire Solomon's 65 percent interest, valued then at about $9 million. The $5 million death benefit paid to Jack, who owned the policy, and covered more than half the obligation. A term policy covered the remaining $4 million. (Where valuation and coverage do not line up exactly, an installment note from Jack to Solomon's estate can bridge the difference.) Solomon's family would have received the proceeds in cash, and Jack would have taken full ownership of a business he already knew how to run, with no bank loan and no outside investor under time pressure. The transition would have closed quickly because the capital was already positioned for the purpose.

Chapter 5 described this structure for funding a buy-sell. Solomon had it in place, and it did the work the chapter said it would.

Function Two: Growth Capital for the Partner Who Owns the Policy
Jack owned the policy, and the cash value inside it was his to use. When an expansion opportunity arrived, Jack borrowed against the policy's cash value. The funds were tax-free, available on the deal's timeline, and required no underwriting and no personal guarantees. Jack solely funded the expansion, increasing his ownership share of the business.

Borrowing against the cash value reduced the policy's death benefit, which still had to fund the buy-sell on Solomon's life. Jack covered the gap with a term policy on Solomon. The term premium cost less than the interest on a comparable bank loan, and the policy loan came with none of a bank's restrictions: no covenants, no personal guarantee, and no limits on how Jack ran the business. The all-in cost of funding the expansion was lower, the business stayed unencumbered, and the buy-sell stayed fully funded throughout.

Function Three: The Buyout and the Hand-Off

Solomon retired first. Once the business changed hands and the buy-sell obligation ended, Jack no longer needed the policy on Solomon's life, so he transferred it to Solomon.

A policy transferred for value can lose its tax-free death benefit, but a transfer to the insured is one of the explicit exceptions in a partnership, so the policy passed to Solomon without a tax liability. Jack's buy-sell tool was now Solomon's asset, with its accumulated cash value and death benefit intact. From here, the policy stopped serving the partnership and started serving Solomon.

He could keep the policy in his own name, where he could borrow the cash value for his own use, or move it into an irrevocable trust, where the death benefit would sit outside his taxable estate. The trust can still borrow against the cash value, but the proceeds have to serve the beneficiaries, not Solomon. The cash value is not frozen. It is redirected, from the owner to the heirs.

Function Four: Funding a Roth Conversion

After retirement, Solomon owned the policy and in his early retirement years, before Social Security and required minimum distributions began, he was in a low tax bracket. He converted pre-tax retirement assets to a Roth account.

The conversion creates a tax bill. Paying it from the retirement account being converted shrinks the amount that reaches the Roth, and selling investments to cover it can trigger capital gains. He borrowed the conversion tax from the policy's cash value instead, tax-free, and let the full pre-tax balance move into the Roth.

The Roth allowed Solomon and his beneficiaries to withdraw funds tax-free for the rest of their lives. That benefit came from the conversion itself. The policy did not create it; it supplied the cash that made the conversion possible without draining the account being converted.

Function Five: Estate Liquidity at Death
By his mid-seventies, Solomon's remaining goal for the policy was no longer personal access but estate liquidity for his heirs. He gifted the policy into an ILIT. Because he was transferring an existing policy, the three-year survival rule applied: the death benefit would only sit outside his estate if he lived three years past the gift.

Solomon retired at 66 and lived to 82, well beyond the three-year window. The policy continued to grow, and the death benefit was worth $5.8 million at his death. It paid to the trust outside the taxable estate and income-tax-free.

Chapters 9 and 11 described this structure for pre-positioning estate liquidity in an irrevocable trust. It closed Solomon's plan.

How Each Function Plays Out by Entity
The mechanics of Solomon's policy were the same regardless of entity type. The tax treatment around each function shifted with the structure, and those shifts compound across decades. The table summarizes the differences across the two structural categories.

Across all five functions, the policy mechanics are nearly identical regardless of entity. The death benefit, the loans, the transfers all work the same way. What changes is the tax treatment at a few specific points, and almost all of it falls on the C-corp side. The table shows where the entity matters and where it does not.

Function	Pass-Through (Partnership, LLC, S-Corp)	C-Corp
Buy-sell at death	Cross-purchase preserves basis step-up under Section 1014. Premium is not deductible at the entity or the owner level.	Same mechanics, but redeeming from a C-corp raises accumulated earnings tax considerations on retained cash value.

Function	Pass-Through (Partnership, LLC, S-Corp)	C-Corp
Liquidity (policy loan)	Loan is tax-free at the policy level. Proceeds reach the owner without a taxable event, whether the policy is held by the entity or individually.	Same mechanics. If the C-corp owns the policy, getting the proceeds out to the owner triggers dividend rules and needs planning.
Partner buyout / hand-off	Transfer to the insured is tax-free, and the partnership exception covers transfers between partners along the way.	No partnership exception. The hand-off is subject to C-corp distribution rules and must be structured to avoid a constructive dividend.
Roth conversion bridge	Conversion is at the owner level. The policy loan funds the conversion tax personally.	No difference. Entity type does not touch this function.
Estate liquidity at death	ILIT ownership keeps the death benefit outside the taxable estate. The business interest gets a step-up at death, reducing heirs' capital gains.	Same. C-corp stock also gets a step-up, and QSBS may exclude gain if the holding-period and other tests were met.

Solomon's business was taxed as a partnership, which is why the hand-off in Function Three passed tax-free under the partnership and insured exceptions rather than through C-corp redemption rules. The policy was the same. The partnership structure was the mechanic that made the tax-free transfer possible.

One structure adapted to every function the book described. That is the capstone's first argument. The second is that no structure is independent of the entity that houses it. Solomon and Jack had the right policy in the right entity and served five functions across the 34-year life of the contract.

Insuring the Plan, Not Just the Things

Every business owner insures the things: the buildings, the inventory, the trucks, the liability. Those risks are familiar and the premiums are the cost of doing business. Solomon did all of that too. What set his plan apart was that he also insured the structure underneath the wealth itself, the single policy that funded the buyout, supplied capital for an expansion and a conversion, and delivered estate liquidity at his death.

The things on the balance sheet had clear replacement costs and were insured without a second thought. The plan that decided what happened to Solomon's wealth, his family, and his business across 34 years was the part most owners never insure at all.

Integration Check: Closing the Book

1. Do my protection, retirement, and benefit structures feed my estate plan, or will they have to be unwound to function?
2. Is my buy-sell coordinated with my succession and exit plan, or are they separate documents that have never been read side by side?
3. Is the wealth I have moved onto my personal balance sheet positioned for both the sale and the estate, not just one?
4. If a buyer arrives tomorrow, would my pre-sale, succession, and estate plans be executed as one plan?
5. Is there a single advisor who has signed off on all of it together?

Chapter 12: Choosing an Advisor Who Sees the Whole Picture

Every structure in this book has a tax, legal, or insurance dimension, and each one connects to the others. The salary decision shapes the retirement plan. The retirement plan shapes the exit. The exit shapes the estate. What you need is not four separate answers to four separate questions. You need one person who sees how they fit together, and whose job is the fit itself.

That person is rare, because the financial industry is built around products, and products are sold by specialists. The CPA, the attorney, the actuary, and the insurance professional are each genuinely good at their piece. But competence in a lane is not the same as ownership of the road. None of them is paid to manage the intersection, and the intersection is where the plan is won or lost.

What to Look For

The advisor who can do this work is not defined by a single credential. A CPA, an attorney, an insurance professional, or a planner can each grow into the role, but only if they think past their own product. What distinguishes them is not what they sell. It is what they ask about before they sell anything.

The right advisor starts with the whole picture: the entity, the people, the retirement plan, the buy-sell, the exit horizon, and the estate, and how each one constrains the others. They notice that the salary figure caps the retirement plan, that the trust funding competes with gifts already in motion, that the buy-sell and the estate plan have to agree on a number. They are looking at the seams, because the seams are where value is won or lost.

A product specialist answers the question you bring them. An advisor who sees the whole picture tells you which question you should have asked. That is the difference, and it is the one worth paying for.

The Advisor Profile

The advisor who plays this role may have trained as any of these, but in this role, they are not acting as your CPA, attorney, or actuary. They:

- Understand all of those domains at a strategic level without practicing in any of them
- Hold a fiduciary standard
- Disclose their compensation whether by fee, commission, or both
- Coordinate with the existing professional team rather than replacing it

The relationship includes the non-operator spouse. If the spouse meets the advisor only after a death or incapacity event, the relationship starts from zero at the worst possible moment. Annual reviews should include both spouses. The structures in this book outlive the working years, and the spouse who survives the owner is the one who lives with them.

That advisor may already be on the team. The gate and the scorecard below indicate where the gaps are.

Coordination Gate

The questions below run before the scorecard, not alongside it. They establish whether the planning has a coordinator. A high score on individual structures does not equal a coordinated plan.

Answer each question yes or no.

1. Is there one advisor who has reviewed my entity structure, qualified plan design, group benefit carve-outs, buy-sell agreement, estate plan, and exit strategy as a single coordinated plan within the last twelve months?
2. Does that advisor know my CPA, my estate attorney, my insurance professional, and my plan actuary, and have they spoken to each other about my plan in the same twelve-month window?
3. Is that advisor's compensation structured so the recommendation is driven by my plan, not by a product sale?
4. Does my non-operator spouse know who that advisor is and have a relationship with them?

If the answer to any of the four is no, the planning is being managed in pieces regardless of how the scorecard below comes out. The scorecard then measures the quality of the individual pieces, not the quality of the plan.

Advisor Integration Scorecard

Score each item: 2 points if fully addressed, 1 if partially, 0 if not. Section subtotals point to the act where the planning is weakest.

FOUNDATION (Acts I–II)		**__ /10**
Entity Structure	Has my entity type been reviewed against current income, exit timeline, and estate size in the last 2 years?	__ /2
Key Person Coverage	Is key person coverage sized against actual revenue exposure and replacement cost?	__ /2
Buy-Sell	Is my buy-sell agreement funded for both death and disability with current valuations?	__ /2
Continuity	Does a written 72-hour plan exist, and does my spouse know where it is?	__ /2

Retention	Do I have a funded retention structure for my most critical employees?	__ /2
EXTRACTING VALUE (Act III)		**__ /10**
Qualified Plans	Am I contributing the maximum tax-deductible amount through a stacked plan design?	__ /2
Plan Insurance	Has anyone evaluated life insurance inside my qualified plan for estate planning?	__ /2
Group Benefits	Do I have an executive carve-out with enhanced GI limits and disability definitions?	__ /2
Disability	Do I have all three layers: personal, group LTD, and business overhead expense?	__ /2
Compen-sation	Is my salary optimized for qualified plan contributions, not just payroll tax minimization?	__ /2
EXIT AND ESTATE (Act IV)		**__ /14**
Valuation	Has a formal business valuation been conducted in the last 2–3 years?	__ /2
Exit Plan	Do I have a written exit strategy with a timeline and tax modeling?	__ /2
Pre-Sale	Have we evaluated CLTs, QSBS, entity restructuring, or premium-financed ILITs?	__ /2
Insurability	Has insurability been confirmed on every person the plan depends on, with tentative offers where appropriate?	__ /2
Estate Liquidity	Is there life insurance outside my taxable estate sized to the estate tax liability?	__ /2
Equalization	If the business goes to one heir, is there an equalization plan for the others?	__ /2

Spouse Readiness	Does my non-operator spouse have access to all accounts, policies, and advisor contacts?	__ /2
CROSS-CUTTING		**__ /4**
Borrowing	Do I have established borrowing capacity (LOC, policy loans, securities-based lending)?	__ /2
Section 199A	Has the QBI deduction been evaluated and optimized?	__ /2
TOTAL SCORE		**__ /38**

33–38	The structures are well-built. Coordination above is the variable that determines whether they work together. Review annually.
24–32	Gaps exist among the structures. Some involve windows that are closing.
15–23	The plan is fragmented at the structure level. Multiple opportunities are being missed.
Below 15	The plan is being managed in pieces. The cost of fragmentation compounds.

If your score surprised you, then a conversation is worth pursuing.

Where to Start

The structures in this book are not equally urgent. The order below reflects which decisions cannot wait.

1. A partner and no funded buy-sell. Seven-figure exposure, five-figure annual cost to close.
2. An estate above the exemption with no insurance outside it. Health, exemption levels, and premiums all

move against the owner over time, with a 40 percent estate tax at the finish line.

3. A potential sale within five years. Entity restructuring, CLTs, QSBS, and premium financing all need lead time.
4. A payroll-company 401(k) with stable income above $350,000. The default plan captures a fraction of what a profit-sharing or cash-balance layer could contribute, often a six-figure annual deduction left on the table.
5. Disability coverage that does not cover all three exposures: personal income, the gap above the individual policy cap, and business overhead. Disability is the most likely insurable event of working life and the least insured against.
6. Uninsured key person risk. A large exposure that can be resolved with a relatively small premium.

Reality Check

Every planning window in this book narrows with time. Most owners discover this after the window has closed. Insurability closes first and without warning, since a single health event can take it. The QSBS clock takes five years to run, so the stock has to be in place long before the sale. And every year an appreciating asset stays in the estate, more of its growth is exposed to the 40 percent tax that moving it earlier would have avoided.

Conclusion

This book asked the owner to do four things. Treat the business and the household as two balance sheets that share an owner. Recognize that the entity decision made years ago may no longer fit the business today. Install the structures that move wealth from the business to the household in a tax and cost efficient manner. Delegate one person to best connect the pieces of the puzzle.

None of the four is technical. The technical work belongs to the specialists. These four are the owner's alone.

An owner who finishes this book and changes nothing has lost nothing yet. The loss comes later, in what was never captured: the partner who dies and the buy-sell pays on a stale valuation, the sale that closes while the entity election from 2012 quietly costs seven figures, the founder who is gone before the surviving spouse has ever met the advisor.

None of that is bad luck. Each one is a decision that was available years earlier and never made. The structures in this book are not complicated to understand. They are only easy to postpone, because the day they are needed is always somewhere in the future, until it is not.

The work is the same work that built the business: see the whole picture, decide early, and put the structure in before it is needed. The owner who built something worth protecting already knows how to do this. The only question left is whether the plan that holds it will be built with the same discipline as the business it is meant to protect.

These decisions are not urgent because they are dramatic. They are urgent because they are easy to defer. Nothing breaks when they are postponed, which is exactly why they get postponed, until the day they cannot be made at all.

The infrastructure goes in years ahead of the need. By the time the need arrives, the window has already closed.

Build the Fortress.

The Financial Fortress Series

Across every stage where wealth is built, captured, and transferred, the Financial Fortress series applies one discipline: coordinated structure, installed before it is realized it is needed.

Financial Fortress: Building a Retirement Plan for Market Risk, Taxes, Inflation, and Life is the first volume. It addresses households approaching or in retirement, where the work is converting accumulated assets into income that survives market sequence risk, tax change, inflation, and a long life.

Financial Fortress for Business Owners: Extract Value through Entity Structure, Protection, Benefits, and Exit, is the second volume. It addresses the owner of a closely held business, where wealth is concentrated in a single illiquid asset and the planning work is moving that wealth onto the personal balance sheet on terms the owner controls.

The third volume of Financial Fortress addresses young savers and accumulators. It provides a strong foundation for personal finances on topics relevant to young professionals.

The planning problems change with the life stage. The discipline that captures the wealth at each stage does not.

The published volumes are available at major retailers.

Additional resources are available at www.FinancialFortress.net.

REGULATORY DISCLAIMER

General

This book is for informational and educational purposes only and does not constitute investment, legal, tax, accounting, or insurance advice. The views expressed are those of the author and do not necessarily reflect the opinions or positions of Triathlon Partners LLC. The mention of Triathlon Partners LLC in this book is for informational purposes only and should not be construed as an endorsement, recommendation, or solicitation of its services or of any specific investment, security, insurance contract, or strategy. Readers should consult with qualified financial, tax, legal, and insurance professionals before implementing any strategy discussed herein.

Adviser Registration and Author Compensation

Triathlon Partners LLC is a registered investment adviser with the State of Connecticut. Registration as an investment adviser does not imply any level of skill or training. The author is the founder of Triathlon Partners LLC, which operates as both a registered investment adviser and an independent insurance brokerage. The author and the firm may receive advisory fees, insurance commissions, or other compensation in connection with the kinds of products and structures discussed in this book. The author may have a financial interest in the investments, insurance contracts, or strategies discussed. Readers considering any structure should compare offers from multiple licensed professionals and verify compensation arrangements before acting.

Investment and Insurance Risk

Investing involves risk, including the potential loss of principal. Past performance is not indicative of future results. Structured products, annuities, insurance contracts, real estate exchanges, and other strategies discussed may involve market risk, credit risk, liquidity constraints, tax implications, and complexity that may not be appropriate for all investors. Insurance guarantees are subject to the claims-paying ability of the issuing insurer. Insurance product features, pricing, underwriting standards, crediting rates, fees, and policy provisions vary by carrier and by policy form. Specific premium-to-benefit ratios and cash-value figures shown in case studies are illustrative and do not represent quotes from any specific carrier or policy. Modified Endowment Contract, transfer-for-value, Section 7702, and other tax-code considerations apply to specific structures and require professional review.

Illustrations and Forward-Looking Projections

Projected values, illustrative returns, growth rates, and policy performance figures shown in this book are hypothetical, based on assumed rates of return and tax treatment in effect at the time of writing. Actual results will differ. Insurance policy illustrations are not guarantees. Non-guaranteed elements may change and could be lower than illustrated. Indexed and variable insurance products carry distinct risks and limitations not fully described in case study form. Any examples of investment strategies, case studies, or financial outcomes discussed in this book are for illustrative purposes only and may not reflect actual results or be suitable for any particular individual.

Tax Law Currency

Tax figures, thresholds, exemptions, brackets, statutory rates, contribution limits, and code-section references cited in this book reflect federal law in effect at the time of writing. These figures are revised periodically by Congress, the Treasury Department, and the Internal Revenue Service. State and local tax treatment varies by jurisdiction and is generally not addressed. Tax laws and regulations are subject to change, sometimes retroactively. Readers should verify current figures and applicable law with a qualified tax professional before acting.

Strategy-Specific Complexity

Certain strategies discussed in this book, including but not limited to premium-financed life insurance, split-dollar arrangements under either the economic benefit or loan regime, deferred sales trusts, charitable lead trusts, qualified small business stock under Section 1202, Section 731 partnership distributions, Section 79 group term carve-outs, and irrevocable life insurance trusts, carry significant complexity, regulatory requirements, and risks not exhaustively addressed in case study form. These structures require coordinated legal, tax, actuarial, and insurance counsel before implementation and are not appropriate for all owners.

Qualified retirement plan designs discussed in this book, including safe-harbor 401(k), profit-sharing, cross-tested, and cash balance plans, are subject to the Employee Retirement Income Security Act and ongoing administrative, fiduciary, and non-discrimination requirements. Plan installation and operation require qualified actuarial, ERISA legal, and third-party administrative support. Cross-tested, cash balance, and combined plan designs are subject to annual testing and may produce different outcomes than illustrated.

No Representations; No Liability

Neither the author, the publisher, nor Triathlon Partners LLC makes any representations or warranties as to the accuracy, completeness, or timeliness of the information contained herein, and assumes no liability for any loss arising from its use. Specific entity structures, insurance contracts, tax elections, and planning techniques discussed in this book are presented for educational purposes and are not recommendations to enter into any such arrangement. Suitability depends on facts and circumstances unique to each owner and business. References to specific securities, asset classes, products, carriers, or strategies should not be interpreted as recommendations or endorsements.

About the Author

Ira S. Koyner has spent his career on the same question in two settings. For nearly thirty years, as a currency options trader at large global banks, the question was how to structure a position so a correct view paid asymmetrically, and a wrong view cost less than it should. As the founder of Triathlon Partners LLC, the question has been the same, applied to the personal balance sheets of business owners and pre-retirees.

Triathlon Partners is a registered investment adviser and independent insurance brokerage built on a single conviction: coordination across professionals and products is how a plan captures its benefits and absorbs its surprises. It is the same asymmetric payoff the preface described, applied to a household instead of an investment.

He holds a degree from the Wharton School of Business at the University of Pennsylvania. He lives in Connecticut with his family.

www.TriathlonPartners.com
www.TheOriginalIRA.com
www.FinancialFortress.net

Triathlon Partners LLC is a registered investment adviser in the State of Connecticut. This book is for informational purposes only and does not constitute an offer of advisory services.

www.ingramcontent.com/pod-product-compliance
Lightning Source LLC
LaVergne TN
LVHW022228200926
848481LV00006B/2173